A GLORIOUS Future

A GLORIOUS *Future*

LEARN ABOUT THE AMAZING PROMISE
THAT INSURES YOU WILL HAVE A HAPPY
AND REWARDING LIFE

GEORGE DURRANT

spring creek
BOOK COMPANY
Provo, Utah

ISBN 978-1-932898-90-3
e. 2

Published by:
Spring Creek Book Company
P.O. Box 50355
Provo, Utah 84605-0355

www.springcreekbooks.com

Cover design © Spring Creek Book Company

Printed in the United States of America
10 9 8 7 6 5 4 3 2 1
Printed on acid-free paper

Library of Congress Control Number: 2007942882

DEDICATION

To my beloved Marilyn,
who has been and will be forever
the best part of my glorious future.

Contents

CHAPTER 1

Here Is Wishing You A Glorious Future

"Would you like to have a glorious future?" I ask.

"Sure!" you reply.

"Then: 'Seek ye first the kingdom of God, and his righteousness; and all these things shall be added unto you.'" (Matt 6:33)

"Is it as simple as that?" you ask.

"It is as simple as that," I reply.

"Tell me more," you ask.

"Read on," I reply.

The Greatest Challenge And The Boldest Promise

Applying this profoundly important scripture is the key that unlocks the door to your "glorious future."

The message of this book encourages you to live the most far-reaching of all commandments: *"Seek ye first the kingdom of God and his righteousness . . ."*

This insures that you will receive, into your life, the blessings of the boldest promise ever made to us by the Lord: *". . . and all these things shall be added unto you."*

This commandment and promise is a spiritual example of "one size fits all." It covers every aspect, situation, opportunity and challenge of life. Under its far-reaching umbrella can be found the

1

solution to all of life's problems and the wisdom and power to live life abundantly and to have a glorious future.

To illustrate:

A young man held a small, live bird in his hand. Desiring to embarrass the village wise man, he asked, "Is the bird I hold in my hand alive or dead?"

If the wise man said it was dead, the young man would open his hand and the bird would fly away. If the wise man said the bird was alive, the young man would squeeze the bird to death and drop it to the ground.

The wise man replied, "The answer to your question is in your own hand."

So it is with your future. Your future is in your hands. And, if you are willing to put your hand into the hand of God, you will have a glorious future.

During the darkest days of World War II, when London was being bombed night and day, King George quoted these words to the British people:

"I said to the man who stood at the gate of the new year, 'Give me a light that I may travel safely into the unknown.' He replied, 'Go out into the darkness and put your hand into the hand of God. For that is better than a light and safer than a known way.'"

God has told you how to put your hand into His. He did so when He invited you to "Seek ye first the kingdom of God, and his righteousness . . ."

And then He made you the boldest promise ever made—

"...and all these things shall be added unto you."

You say, "This all sounds amazing, but how do I know if this promise will really be realized, and how do I make it work for me?"

"Read on," I reply.

CHAPTER 2

This Promise Really Works

"Does this promise made in this bold statement really work?" you ask.

"It sure does," I reply.

"How do you know it works?" you ask.

"Read on."

Exhibit One

My dear friend, Dale LeBaron, told me the following story:

The Night We Put Our Hands into the Hand of God

In the 1940s my father called my mother and us eight children into the kitchen and asked us to all sit down around the table in the small farmhouse in Western Alberta, Canada. The family was in the midst of very difficult financial times.

My father told the family that he had talked to the bishop that day, and now had a matter to discuss with the family. In a most serious tone, he advised us that the only way to do what the bishop had asked was for each of the family to be willing to make great sacrifices. As we all listened with great eagerness he said, "The bishop has asked Homer to serve a mission for the Church."

All eyes fell on Homer, the oldest of the eight children. Homer seemed to desire to smile, but could not quite do so.

Father continued, "The bishop said that for Homer to go, we would all have to finance him at a cost of some seventy dollars per month. You all know that we are just barely able to survive financially. For us to come up with that much money would mean that all of us would have to sacrifice more than we have ever done before."

We already knew what it was like to go without. For the past several years we could scarcely even afford second-hand clothes. Only the family cow, the chickens, and the vegetable garden had enabled us to live. Seventy dollars seemed like an amount far beyond our fondest hope.

· Father and Mother knew it would not be smart to demand, without our consent, such an impossible financial commitment. After several seconds of silence, Mother took a deep breath and then spoke, "We can do it. Homer can go. We can do it. Somehow we can come up with the money it will take."

Father looked at her, then with moistened eyes looked first at Homer and then at each of us other seven children. Then he spoke, "How do you all feel? You will have to each work harder on the farm. You won't have much money for doing anything fun."

He then called each of us by name, from the oldest to the next oldest, and asked, "Are you willing to make the sacrifices necessary to send Homer seventy dollars per month?" Each one of us nodded in agreement. The chairs were then moved back and the family knelt in the most fervent prayer we had ever uttered.

I'll never forget even one small detail of that experience in our little home. I was fourteen years old at the time. I had never before felt what I felt then as I committed to my father that I was willing to do whatever it took for my brother to serve a mission.

Things were never again the same for us. That night our family was transformed in a wonderful way. Homer served a most rewarding mission in France for two and a half years.

For the first several months that he was gone we all made the pledged sacrifices. But gradually, almost unnoticed little miracles began to occur. Things began to financially turn around on our little farm. We did not become rich, but we were never again strapped for money as we had been in the past.

But more than money was involved. Our family was just different after that. Oh, we still had problems. However, miraculously there were always solutions. I will forever be grateful for that quiet night in Canada that changed everything that matters for me.

In my mature years, I served as a counselor in a stake presidency to this humble man of God who told me this story from his childhood. While working with him, I often marveled at his wisdom and his commitment to truth. His faith and knowledge of sacrifice enabled him to lead a multitude on this continent and in Africa to become closer to the eternal values of life. He and his wife, after nearly 50 years of marriage, are more in love than ever before. His children revere the two of them. Truly, "...all these things" that Christ promised have miraculously been added unto him. His life and the life of his family have been, and continue to be, glorious.

When Christ made this, the boldest promise ever made to man, He did so in a setting of explaining how money or worldly possessions cannot buy the miracle of "the beauty of the lilies." My friend truly lived a life wherein the Lord had blessed him with blessings as beautiful and indescribable as that of the lilies.

Exhibit Two

The Amazing Packard Family

The children came so fast. But that was just what the Packard parents desired. It was just that the farm was so small and prices were so low that the family could scarcely see, apart from their faith in God, how they could survive. There was not much work in Boise Valley and the wages were low. And raising fifteen children (and another soon to be born) required more money than they could earn.

Then a golden opportunity came into view. Brother Packard

was a finish carpenter and knew much of the construction trade. There was an opportunity to work on Wake Island. A construction company from the area had received a contract to build an airfield there. They needed men for a year.

The young couple put pen to paper and decided that if he went for the year, they would be able to pay off the farm. With their hearts breaking at their separation, he departed early in the year 1941 for Wake Island.

The only good thing was that the money problem that had plagued them for so long was now solved.

Then, in December 1941, the Japanese blew up their dream. They invaded Wake Island and Brother Packard was taken prisoner. There was no word of his life or death. There was no way to get word.

Soon the money stopped. Now the family was in total jeopardy. The father was gone. There was the disconsolate mother, perhaps a widow, and sixteen children with very little income. There was no way the mother could make the farm payments.

At first, Sister Packard was in complete despair. But then she came to herself. She came to her God, and a feeling of hope began to faintly shine in her heart. And with this treasured hope, she began to know that all things were possible and that the future would be bright.

She knew that she and her husband had always sought the kingdom of God first. That foundation of her faith in God would not let her down now. Instead, He would somehow lift her up. She decided to leave sorrow and despair behind, cast her burdens on the Lord, and get on with her life. She knew in her heart, though others doubted, that her husband was alive and would come back. But when? And what to do until then? She did not know all the answers, but she knew the Lord and knew that all would be well. From the moment she put her hand into the hand of God and walked out into the darkness, things began to happen.

There was a lady in her area who sold clothes door to door. Sister Packard asked if she could help her with this business. Sister Packard, mother of sixteen, with her radiant and loving personality, was able to arrange her time so that she could leave her children for a few hours each day and call on the mothers in the area. People needed what she had to sell. Plus, she was a super salesperson. Food was again on the table in more than meager amounts. The children rallied around and cared for the farm. Now the farm payments were made on time and even earlier.

Two years later the family received the glorious news that their father was still alive in a prison camp in China and, hopefully, he would soon return home. The thoughts of his family and prayers for them had sustained this faithful father through an almost unbearable time. A more glorious reunion has never been known than the one when Brother Packard, Sister Packard, and the sixteen children were once again back together and resumed their lives on the now paid-for farm.

In the years that followed, the Packards had one more child, making a total of seventeen children. They now have 119 grandchildren and 443 great-grandchildren. They have a total of 1171 blood descendants—and with spouses, their posterity now totals 1475. Never has there been a family so filled with love and faith as are the descendants of these glorious people. Their numbers are great, and even more remarkable, the quality of their souls is glorious.

Exhibit Three

A Troubled Couple Seek a Better Way

A prominent young couple married in the temple and it seemed a successful marriage and a glorious future were almost a guarantee. However, things soon began to fall apart. They did not see eye to eye on a number of little things and on many big things. After a time, both felt they had fallen completely out of love. They tried marriage counseling. It helped a little, but not enough.

Then, they each, separately and together, decided that if they would seek the kingdom of God first, all the other differences would be resolved. They began to experiment on the words, "Seek ye first the kingdom of God." They planted these words in their hearts. Things began to change. Others, when in their presence, noticed that their relationship was different than it had been previously. They were complimentary to each other. They were considerate of each other. The spirit of the Lord filled their joint countenance. That was many years ago. They have since struggled with some of their children. However, time, as it so often does, healed these wounds. Their children brought honor to their name. This couple's love for each other and their service to their God has caused many to admire them and to strive to be more like them. *All these promised things* have become part of them.

Exhibit Four

Seeking the Kingdom at Home

A certain woman was a beloved and respected woman in her ward and in the entire stake. She was often called to serve in leadership positions. Many who worked with her admired her kindness, the way she did so much for so many, and for her encouragement to others. She was a true builder of the kingdom of God.

However, her husband refused to set foot in church. She had tried over the years to encourage him to become "active." But he resented her interfering in his life. She began to have a disdain for his attitude and for him, and was often critical of his lifestyle. It was a joy for her to be out among the people, succeeding in helping others who appreciated her. However, there was not much joy at home.

In an interview with the stake president, she asked him what he felt she should do about her marriage. He advised her to be more fervent in building the kingdom of God in her own home by treating her husband the way she treated those with whom she served in her church calling.

The lights went on for her. She had been so gracious out in the church. Now, in her home, she added an even greater dose of this graciousness to him. The details of just what she did are not as important as the fact that her desires changed. She loved him. She honored him. She praised him. She nurtured him. None of this was to manipulate him. She sincerely desired him to know of her love for him, regardless of whether or not he returned to church activity.

Miracles, almost greater than the calming of a storm-tossed sea, began to occur—quiet little miracles that change a person from the inside out. A few months later, the man appeared at the office of the stake president. There, in a private interview, the man asked, "President, do you think the church house would fall down if I came back inside?"

He came back, and the church house still stands, and so does he. And so does she—taller than ever. They have a glorious life together, now and forever.

Note: Space will not allow me to list the other 1,000 plus exhibits I could list.

So I say to you, "Your future is in your hands as you put your hands into the hand of God. 'Seek ye first the kingdom of God, and his righteousness; and all these things shall be added unto you.'" (Matt 6:33)

"Wow!" It really works," you exclaim. Then you ask, "How can I live this commandment and get these blessings?"

"Read on," I reply.

CHAPTER 3

Seek First The
Kingdom Of God

You just asked, ""How can I live this commandment and get these blessings?"

First you have to find the kingdom of God on the earth and become part of it. Missionaries are now all over the world inviting people to become part of that kingdom. Following are two accounts of people who decided to be baptized so that they could become part of the kingdom of God.

1. A Young Couple in Canada

My wife, Marilyn, and I were on a Church Education Mission in Toronto, Canada. Our supervisor there was Ken Shoesmith. Just writing the name of this noble man causes me to well up with emotion. No person ever helped a missionary couple more than he helped us. But great as he was, he was not quite the equal to his wife Gloria. Gloria fits so well into the word *"glorious,"* as will be seen in the following story:

Setting the Stage

It was in the fall of 1996 and we were traveling by car from Toronto, Canada to Boston for an Area Church Education convention. The autumn leaves were in full bloom and the beauty in every direction was beyond description.

Because we had known Ken and Gloria for a year, we were aware that they had received the full promise, "that all these things shall be added to you." However, it was in this heavenly setting that they related to us the story of how they initially qualified for these glorious blessings.

The following story, in Ken's own words, is how they came to "seek first the kingdom of God."

Before I became a "Mormon" in 1966, I was an active member of another faith. I loved my church. I believed it taught as much correct doctrine as others and that its services of worship were unequaled in other denominations. Unfortunately, I was growing weary of hearing lectures on sociology instead of sermons on the gospel.

At this time we attended the World's Fair and the Mormon Pavilion in New York in August of 1965. We liked the displays, even though I thought many of them were "way out." Imagine Jesus visiting this continent in 34 A.D.!

One of the funniest things to me was the display of the photographs of the Quorum of the Twelve. Apostles in business suits! Ha! Ridiculous! Apostles would wear beautifully exquisite robes. Nevertheless, we were impressed, and my wife bought a Book of Mormon and we took some pamphlets.

As we left New York, Gloria began to read from the "Joseph Smith's Testimony" pamphlet. "Just listen to this," she would say. "Isn't this interesting? It's fantastic."

"Yes, I know," I replied, "I've heard it all before. Don't tell me. I've heard all about that boy going into the woods and seeing a light (here, bursts of laughter) and seeing God and Jesus (here almost uncontrollable fits of laughter)."

Early in September two missionaries came to our door and asked for an appointment. I decided I might as well find out about the "Mormons."

The time arrived and the door bell rang. When I answered it, there stood two young men, Elders Dean Roberts and Scott

Berglund, looking very neat in their trim, dark suits with fedoras sitting on the tops of their heads. I almost laughed then and there! The next thing I knew they were rearranging furniture, having "a word of prayer" and an obviously "pat" dialogue was being thrust upon us. Oh, how I laughed through that first discussion! Only one church with the proper authority? Oh, brother! Tell me another one! Then the kneeling word of prayer. Another discussion? But all I wanted was to know a *little* about their church.

Well, I let them come back, rearrange furniture, pray, and present their material. (I was convinced they must have gone through intensive training to perform as efficiently as they did). What, four more such discussions? I wasn't laughing anymore.

Our first visit to the ward chapel was almost disastrous. We were used to a beautiful church—carpet, lovely stained glass windows, altar, exquisitely carved wood, pipe organ, choir, pomp and ceremony, no talking, and reverence. We encountered a very plain building, and noisy irreverence. As we left, I said to my wife, "How could we ever regularly go to that church?" However, the farther away we drove, the less we thought of the noise and the more we thought of the friendliness, the handshaking, the interest people had in us, and the love people seemed to have for each other.

By now we were living most of the principles suggested. I was very busy and couldn't get into the Book of Mormon, although I was reading the pamphlets. Gloria, however, was really going through the Book of Mormon.

Following the discussions (held on Friday nights) we would stay up to all hours discussing things, looking up scriptures, trying to sort things out. I couldn't seem to get an answer to my prayers. Sometimes I felt good about praying concerning a question, but sometimes I didn't. We passed two baptismal goal dates. We completed the six discussions and had several more brainstorming sessions, scriptures and doctrine discussions, study sessions from the Book of Mormon, etc.

On November 21, we spoke to the ward bishop. I told him I didn't feel right about many things and couldn't be baptized. Gloria seemed very disappointed. That night, she attended the sacrament service by herself. She had never been so bold in going out on her own like that. I felt so empty as she left, and during the time she was gone. When she came home, she shocked me by announcing, "I'm getting baptized . . . tomorrow night." I was dumbfounded. She told me she knew these things were true and she had to do something about it. Although it upset me, I gave my consent. It was then that I realized that she had had a testimony for some time, but had doubted it because of her great faith in my judgment. In fact, as I look back, I think she had a testimony after reading the Joseph Smith pamphlet in August. She thought that if I didn't think it was true, then there must be something wrong with it. At last, however, the Holy Spirit had prevailed and Gloria took the big step on her own. I attended her baptism and managed to offer the prayer before we entered the chapel. I felt lonely and deserted. It was the first big thing I'd known Gloria to do on her own.

Gloria was baptized on Monday, November 22, 1965. The elders continued to come and discuss my problems and questions. I believed so much of it was true. I'd seen the tremendous change that had taken place in Gloria. One by one, my problems disappeared. I began to have good feelings when I prayed, but I still wasn't "convinced."

There were two events which helped me gain my testimony. On November 14, Stake President Davies was in Hamilton and we were introduced to him as investigators. He was very friendly and sincere but said nothing to try to sway us. Two weeks later at Stake Conference, we met again and he remembered our name— an extremely unusual thing—people always forget or called us Shoestring or Shoelace. But he remembered!

The second event was a visit from the local minister of my former church. He dropped in because he knew we were new in his parish and he wanted to get acquainted. I said, "You've come at the right time. My wife has just joined the Mormon Church and I'm thinking about it." He was most concerned and interested and wanted to know what had attracted her to the Mormon Church.

They sat at opposite ends of the coach and debated the matter.

Never had I heard my wife quote scriptures before. Never had she expressed herself so well. I, the learned theologian in the family, (I had taken several religion courses at university), couldn't get a word in edgewise. I almost fell off my chair. I couldn't believe how strong she was.

Finally, all my arguments fell away. I was filled with a wonderful peace. I knew that what I was doing was right and I began to look forward to my baptism. From this point on, praying was much easier. Through prayer now, as well as intellectually, I knew the Church was true. I followed my plan and was baptized on Sunday, January 2, 1966.

As we rode along we talked of Ken and Gloria's life and their thirty years in the Church. A year and some months after their baptism, while Gloria was pregnant, they drove in a non-air-conditioned car in the heat of summer from Toronto to Salt Lake City to have their marriage sealed for all eternity. They have raised a glorious family. They have each served in many callings in the Church. Ken has been a bishop, a stake president, and a sealer in the temple. He left his position as an elementary school principal to become the coordinator of seminaries and institutes in southern Ontario. But more than all that, they are "Saints." Marilyn and I have never known better.

2. A Fifteen-Year-Old Young Woman in Ireland

My granddaughter, Jessica, recently returned from her mission in Ireland. She told me of a fifteen-year-old young Irish girl, Joanne McCabe. I was so impressed that I have included the account of this amazing young convert as she herself, Joanne, recorded it in her personal journal.

Feb. 18, 2007

Guess what??? Today I came home from training and there were two girl missionaries in my house. Girls—like, I'm used to seeing boys, but girls . . . that's new! It made me laugh. I kinda heard the gist of what they were talking about but didn't really catch much. They said something about some dude they called Joseph Smith, though the story actually seemed interesting. From what I gather he's some kind of prophet or something and had something to do with the Book of Mormon. I dunno much about their religion except that they are not allowed to drink tea and coffee. They are kinda strict, too, from what I heard. Yeah, I don't think I'd ever do something like that! I'm not even into religion. And anyway, I certainly wouldn't go to their religion because I heard it is too strict and I wouldn't change myself for anything 'cause I'm happy as I am, ha ha. But I do think what they do is cool. For them. They have been coming around to the house for years but most of the time it's just men. Actually, it's always men. What are they doing? I mean, what's the point? They are so holy and stuff! They seem funny and stuff, but not a hope would I do something like that...

Later

Today the missionaries were at my house again. They seem really funny but, like, I don't understand what they are all about! I mean, all the time I see them they seem to be talking about Jesus and stuff. They're probably nuns or something. But they are, like, 20 or something. Who wants to be a nun at 20? Ha ha. No, there's nothing wrong with nuns, but, like, I kinda feel sorry for them 'cause they are both really pretty and stuff! Yeah, but today I over heard a couple of things and it seems interesting, but I'm not sure. I wouldn't minds learning or listening to it once or twice though. I can't see myself getting into it, though. It's just not me. There's too much involved in that religion! Too many rules! So I could never see myself getting into it. Not a hope.

March 4, 2007

Guess what has changed??? EVERYTHING!! Well, where do

I start?? Okay, remember those missionaries I told you about?. They are actually cool. They came to teach me today for the first time! They taught me the Restoration and just explained about the Book of Mormon. It turns out that the Church of Jesus Christ was restored through the prophet Joseph Smith and that the Book of Mormon was translated by Joseph Smith. Cool, huh? It turns out he was really young, like fourteen or something, and he was praying to know what church was true and he got a really good answer. He was told that he could find out for himself by asking God. He read this in the Bible and when he did then he got a really cool answer. I wonder if it is all true, though! If it was it would mean so much to me. It would be life changing!!! But I'm a bit iffy on it . . .

First day at church!!
What can I say? I actually went to church today! I didn't think I would but I did. And funny enough I actually enjoyed it! I like these missionaries but I don't know which is which because I always get the two mixed up. Church was good today and my lesson with the sisters was kinda worth thinking about!! They taught about apostasy and everything and I think the one whose name is Sister Durrant drew a little diagram on the black board. But what they said really made sense and it's only right that we should have a modern-day prophet. What they say makes so much sense, it's unreal. They talked a bit about the way in which the Church is true and stuff and about priesthood and what the Church has to make it the true church. They asked me to pray tonight and ask if it is true and if I find out it's true, will I be baptized? I mean the minute they said it I thought, of course I would be baptized into the Church if I found out it was true! I mean, wouldn't anyone?

I came home from church today and I spent a while reading the Book of Mormon. I found it a tiny bit boring at the start, but when I got into it I didn't want to put it down. I know this might sound funny, but as I read it I find it to be so true, it's like I know it really happened or something. I don't know, it's kind of weird. But I was talking to my mum a while ago and I told her that if I found it to be true that I would like to be baptized. She was kinda shocked, and said how Pauline (my godmother) would be disappointed and stuff and I told her that if I found out it was true I wouldn't care what anyone else thinks. So then my mum told me to do whatever I thought was right. So it leaves me with one thing to do and that is to pray about it. So that's what I'm about to do in about 15 fifteen minutes. So we'll see how it goes. I'll write about it tomorrow.

Next day!!

Okay, so today I went to school, which was really boring because it's, well . . . school!!! But anyway, I got news. I prayed last night, okay, and asked if the Church was true and all and now I think even more that it is because I felt happy, but weird, because I felt like I already knew it was true. But, like, I don't know what to do about it now. I mean, I know it's true without a doubt, but I kinda think now I wish I didn't know. Because, like, it's ME—JOANNE!! I mean, I'm not even sure how my friends would react if I told them. I still don't believe I'm doing something like this! I mean, it's me!!! Ha ha. I told my mum today that I'm thinking of being baptized and she couldn't believe it because it's me!! Ha ha. I told her not to tell the Sisters yet, though, because I wanted to learn more first, so we will see how that goes. I feel like it's true and stuff, but I mean, will I find it hard? I feel that there is something missing in my life and I think this is it. But I'm kind of iffy on it. Whatever happens, happens!!

March 16, 2007

Okay, I haven't written in ages, so I have lots of scandal. Okay, where do I start? Okay, I'm getting baptized on Saturday week in a lake!!! Ha ha. I'm kinda excited, but nervous at the same time because, like, now I learned about all the changes I have to make, so we will see how that goes, but to be honest I don't care because I believe it is so true. I mean, I have never felt like this in my entire life. And I still can't believe I'm doing something like this. I never thought I would. But funny enough, I am so happy about it. I guess before I thought I had everything I needed, but little did I know!! Like, I thought I had everything. I mean, I get on with everyone in school. I'm, like, into all the school football teams and was just satisfied. But little did I know how little I really had! I mean, I think knowing that the Church of Jesus Christ is on the earth today is the most anybody can ever have. And I'd give up all those things for it. I know I would do it, but I do realize it would be with great difficulty. But there's no doubt in my mind that I would do it. I told Shelly (my best friend for over ten years) about it today and she wasn't really fussed about it. Which was a bit of a surprise. I told my sister, too. It was so funny! She sure knows how to make someone feel relaxed! Ha ha! She was saying, "Make sure you don't drown!"

March 24, 2007

BAPTISM! Ahhh, it's all done and I got baptized and have never been happier! We met at the church first and I got dressed in my whites. So did Joe. Shelly came, too, which was a bit of a surprise because I didn't expect her to. But it was class to see her there. Yeah, we got to Glencarr Lake, anyway, and I was so excited. We took loads of pictures and stuff. It was cool.

But the best part about it was when I came back up from the water. I didn't even feel cold. I just felt amazing and I can't even explain it!! WOW!!! I have never been happier. I mean I did so many things before like winning football cups, and academic awards, but I have never achieved more than what I have achieved today. I know who I am, for starters. I mean, when I used to look in mirrors to admire myself (ha ha) I always knew that something was missing. I knew what I was on the outside, but what my reflection never showed was who I was in the inside. That was because of only one reason, and that was the truth. And the cool bit about it is that I know of the truth not only by the reason but also by the heart. And I mean, as cheesy as it might sound, it is so true.

I'm so grateful for Sister Durrant and Sister Tolman for finding me. What would be me in three years if they didn't?? It's a good thing I don't have to think about that now!! I get freaked out when I do think of it, though. I'm gonna make mistakes, but I feel protected and I know I can ask for forgiveness for those mistakes.

One mistake I hope I never make is the mistake of not believing these things to be true. I love the Church so much and the Book of Mormon and just everything about it. I mean, why wouldn't I?? No one in their right mind who knows it was true wouldn't. I just loved the day so much and I'm still thinking, did it really happen, because it's me and I was so different before!!

My second favorite part of the day was when Sister Durrant sang. Such an amazing singer she is. I love that girl so much. She's class. She and Sister Tolman are everything I would like to be when I'm older. They are just so cool and I love their enthusiasm about teaching!

If I ever go on a mission I want to be at least close to being as good as them. Because praying to be as good as them is asking for too much!! No joke, they are unique missionaries.

So yep, today was and is a day I will always remember for the rest of my life. And I don't think it can be replaced any time soon.

After the church and stuff, me and my mum, dad, and sister all had Chinese and for the first time ever we had a prayer all together. Its was so cool. There's so much more I can write down but it would be too long, but those feelings will always have a special place in my heart, and so will the people who helped this day to happen.

Several weeks later

My friends were all at me again today! I was so upset about it and I'm still raging . . . I don't know how much more of this I can take!! I feel that there is not one person helping me. I just can't even stand straight and those that I need help from I feel that I can't lean on them, but they are just standing beside me! But if there is one thing that helps me stand straight, it is the Book of Mormon. That is the only thing I can turn to because it is so positive. In my opinion it is truly the most true and correct book. I'm so glad I know it is true and that Joseph Smith translated it. I feel lucky that I prayed about it to see if it was true. Because if I hadn't then what would I have in time like this to turn to?

It's so hard right now, though. But I have to make the right choices and follow our Father's Plan because the choices I make here will decide where I will stand in the last day. Even with the Plan for us, we are so lucky. And just because my friends don't want to follow the right path doesn't mean that I have to do the same. I love them so much, though, and always will, but there is nothing I can say that will change their minds. So all I can do is pray for them!

A week later

Today I learned about the temple! WOW!!

In Young Women with the two sisters and Juliette I learned that the temple is the closest place on earth that we can be to our Heavenly Father. That's so cool.

What do I think about the temple? I think the temple is amazing!! Not only is it for the living but it is also for the dead. First I thought it was a bit weird when I heard about it, but now I think that it is cool and that our ancestors need our help and are waiting for us.

The temple is the only place that families can be sealed together as families.

Young Joanne McCabe is on a journey to a glorious future. As she herself knows, it will not be an easy journey. Always seeking first the kingdom of God requires sacrifice and strength. She will receive the strength and she will know the joy of sacrifice. That will make her journey one of pure joy.

A Life-long Quest

Becoming a member of the kingdom of God is the beginning. However, seeking first the kingdom of God throughout your life is the true test. Here are just a few of those who I have known who have been successful in this life-long quest.

A Most Unforgettable Man

Ned Winder passed away recently, but he will never be forgotten. Some of you knew Ned. I wished you all had. Knowing him was quite a joy. All through his life he sought the kingdom of God first about as well as anyone I have ever known. And he did it with such good nature and humor.

I recall many years ago when my family and I drove to Ogden for the state basketball tournament. Our son, Devin, was playing in that tournament. He and his team played Murray High School that day. Murray had a player named Craig Hammer who was a real player. We were fearful that he alone might beat Devin and his Provo High teammates.

At halftime the game was still in doubt. We were beside ourselves with anxiety.

Ned, who attended and was an official at all basketball tournaments for fifty or so years, came over from the scorer's table to the bleachers and talked to Marilyn, our six children who were there, and me. While he was there, he put something in my shirt pocket. I did not look to see what it was, but assumed it was a note expressing kind feelings.

Provo just barely won the game and we were thrilled. It was only after the jubilant celebration that I reached into my pocket and pulled out what I thought would be a note from Ned. And it was a note. It was a fifty-dollar bill. (That would be much more than a hundred-dollar bill now.) At first I thought, "This can't be right. I'm sure he meant to give us five dollars." But then I thought of Ned, and I knew there was no mistake.

After the game, our family went to Marie Callendar's instead of McDonald's. I don't think we were ever as happy before, or since, as we were when we sat there having a delicious dinner paid for by Ned Winder.

I knew that the fifty dollars was no proof that we were Ned's favorite family. He treated everybody like they were his favorites. As I write this, my eyes fill with tears at the memory of this glorious man who loved so dearly the kingdom of God and all the

people who made up that kingdom. What a mighty man was Ned
Winder.

He and his family owned and operated Winder Dairy. As part
of that business they also had a bakery, and, strangely enough, a
cemetery. I can still see Ned smiling and saying, "Drink our milk
and eat our bread and let us bury you when you are dead." Ned had
the finest sense of humor I have ever known and the biggest heart.
He kept you laughing and he made you feel like you could move
a mountain.

I believe Ned was a moderately rich man in matters relating to
money. But he was an immensely rich man in matters related to
mankind. Ned's wife, Gwen, was a glorious jewel. Only she could
have been the perfect mate for Ned. He loved her so dearly and she
him.

I knew only one of Ned's children, Ned Jr. He was as much like
his dad as he could be. No one could be fully like Ned—not even
his own son. But this son was a joy to Ned and Gwen as were all
their other children.

To me, Ned was proof that Christ's great promise was valid.

For so it was then and now, for Ned and his "forever bride."
They will eternally have an even more glorious future. And with
them in the kingdom of heaven, even that glorious place, will be a
bit more cheerful.

A Most Giving Man

Kurt Olsen was another proof of the validity of the Lord's bold
promise. I don't even know where Kurt is now. All I know is that
wherever he is, things are better there by a long ways, than they
would be if Kurt was not there.

He was once mission president in Colombia, South America.
He invited all the missionaries who were serving locally to his home
for Thanksgiving. When they all gathered around the table they
were amazed at the abundance of delicious food that was before
them. They could hardly wait to join their president, his wonderful
wife, and their seven children in this delicious meal.

Just as they were about to begin, Kurt asked for silence so he could say what was in his heart. What he said was something those missionaries and family members will never forget. He said, "There are many people in this city who are much hungrier than any of us have ever been. This day many of them will have little or nothing to eat. Therefore, I propose that we put all this food into small boxes and take it to these people who need it so much."

Those at the table could scarcely believe what they had heard. They hoped it was not true. Maybe he meant take the leftovers to the poor. But that is not what he meant. He meant to take it all. Those who were there began to pack up the food. At first they did so reluctantly. But then they caught the spirit of it, and they have never before or since had such a glorious Thanksgiving as when they took this food to the needy.

Oh, yes! This is the rest of the story! They all came back to the mission home and had some delicious tuna fish sandwiches.

Now I don't advise you to try this at home. Leave things like that to Kurt Olsen. That sort of thing was second nature to him.

He sold me a home once. His wife loved the home and was sad their work required that they move. She wanted someone just right to live there. She would pray and ask the Lord to arrange things so that the next people who came to see the home would be the ones that He wanted to buy it. She prayed that way three times and each of the three times Marilyn and I were the ones who came to her house right after her prayer. But there was a hitch—we could not afford it.

Finally, at the persuasion of his wife, Kurt asked us, "Just how much can you afford?"

I told him and he said, "If that is all you can afford, then that is what we will sell it to you for."

It was a terrible deal for Kurt and so I told him that we could not do that. But he soon had the paperwork drawn up and we had a home.

Now I know that is foolish talk. You can't do business in this world like that. But Kurt could. He knew that the Lord would give him "all these things." But even knowing this, I think Kurt would say, "Please take *all these things* you would give to me, and give them to others who need them more than me." I long to again see Kurt. I know if I can get to the Celestial Kingdom that I will. Kurt will forever have a glorious future because he knew the Lord's command and promise were valid.

A Man for All Seasons

Buddy Richards is a man I don't know as well as I would like. All I know is that he teaches at BYU and that his glorious wife is (or has been) on the City Council in Provo, Utah.

They live in the central part of the city of Provo. I think they moved there when that was all they could afford. However, as the years passed, they could have moved to a newer area of town. That is what most of their fellow professional people did. However, Buddy and his wife could sense how much they were needed in the area. Many Hispanics and other minorities had moved into the neighborhood, which included many single parents and their children.

Buddy was called to be the bishop. The people loved him. They relied on him and Sister Richards. They were the direction everyone looked when they wanted help of any kind.

Maybe after Buddy's service as bishop they would move to a new home. But it wasn't being bishop that caused the people to love Buddy. They loved him just because he was Buddy, just because they trusted him. Just because they knew he loved them. Just because the whole area was made richer with the Richards family living there. Sister Richards ran for, and won, a seat on the city council, where she always spoke up for her area. She brought many blessings to the people.

They still live there in the central part of the city. Buddy is now stake president. I'm sure that is where they will stay until they die. And then there will be a mighty funeral and a flood of tears. I wish I could know Buddy better. In the few times I have seen him, I knew that he had truly received "all these things." They have now and will have forever a glorious future.

He and his wife verify the Savior's words: "Seek ye first the kingdom of God, and his righteousness; and all these things shall be added unto you." (Matt 6:33)

A Woman Who Will Have It All

Mary Walker, or Mary Poppins, as our children call her, lives in England. I first met her when she came to serve a mission in the Yorkshire area of England. I was serving there also. Her family home was just some fifty miles from where she was called to serve. She was kind of a local, full-time missionary.

She was very young then and quite naïve—kind of like the rest of us, only more so. Her faith was as powerful as it was simple.

She spoke in a broad Yorkshire dialect that was difficult for us to understand. However, her love for us and all the people made it so we all understood her perfectly.

She became the companion of Sister Burnham, who later became my wife.

The two of them had remarkable results. They were almost as successful as Wilford Woodruff. I mean, they really were! For several months they brought people to baptism almost every week. Sister Burnham would teach the people and Mary would love them. It was the perfect combination.

I, being a prankster, spotted an article in the newspaper that told of something that had happened in my area some fifty years ago. It told of some Mormon elders who had cut a limb off a tree to make a baseball bat so they could play baseball at an outing they were having in the park. The elders were arrested and fined for their misdeed. I cut off the part about this being fifty years ago and sent it to Sister Walker. I told her that I needed five pounds to pay the fine for cutting the tree. I thought she would recognize that it was a joke. She did not. She promptly sent me the five pounds, which was all she had for the second half of that month.

Then I had the unpleasant task of telling her it was a joke. To her, it was no joke. I was really sorry.

That was the way Mary was. She would give you all that she

had. That is what she did for the Lord. She gave him all that she had. She truly did seek first the kingdom of God.

That was many years ago. In time Sister Burnham and I came home from our missions, got married, and over the years had eight children. Marrying and having a family is exactly what Mary wanted. But it never happened for her. No one came along. Every year or so, she would come across the ocean to visit us. Our children loved her. They called her Mary Poppins. They truly felt that was who she was.

Everybody loved Mary. Through the years she has served so very well in the Church in England. Her church service includes three other full-time missions.

Finally a man came along when they were both in their sixties. We rejoiced to learn that her life-long dream of getting married in the temple had come true. But it was soon obvious that the marriage was a mistake. The two of them tried, but it would not work and they were divorced. Mary was devastated. But it did not slow her down. She kept right on blessing people and treating their children as her own.

I wish you could meet Mary. If you were a non-Mormon you could meet her. She tells every non-Mormon she meets about the Church. She has brought a multitude to the truth. She is still on fire with life.

Last Christmas, we received our annual card from her. She keeps our picture in a prominent place in her home. We are her favorites, along with everybody else she knows.

Mary has truly sought the kingdom of God first. Has she been given "all these things"? She sure has. She has been given "all these things" and much, much more—every new day Mary walks further and further into her glorious future. She gets more than her share from the Lord because He knows she will share it all with everyone she meets.

Mary is the perfect example of the Lord's words: "Seek ye first the kingdom of God, and his righteousness; and all these things shall be added unto you."

You respond to these examples and ask, "I want to be like these people. How do I do it? How do I really seek first the kingdom of God?"

"Read on," I reply.

CHAPTER 4

How Do We Seek The Kingdom Of God First?

You asked, "How do I go about seeking the kingdom of God first?"

That is a little like wanting to write a symphony and asking Beethoven, "How do I write a symphony?" The symphony just has to be inside wanting to get out so much that it is always on your mind. When you have an internal desire to seek the kingdom of God first, no one has to tell you what to do. You just feel it. It is not knowing the parts of what must be done. Rather, it is a vision of knowing the whole of what needs to be done. These internal feelings and yearnings are your prompting motive to seek God's righteousness.

To me, "seeking the kingdom first" is an overriding attitude. It is not being perfect in every detail, it is in wanting to be perfect in the whole of life. It is in having remorse for miss-steps. It is in desiring to change whenever your heart tells you that you are wrong and to increase your effort when your heart tells you that you are right. With such an attitude as part of your very being, you will, in a sense, write a life's symphony in harmony with seeking first the kingdom of God.

I don't feel I've done well in explaining what I mean. So let me illustrate by telling you a bit of my story—of our story—as Marilyn and I have attempted in our own weak way to seek first the kingdom of God.

We met while we served as missionaries in the British Mission. We were in the same mission district for the entire eighteen months of her mission. First we came to respect each other as we shared in the great cause of bringing the gospel to our beloved friends in England. Toward the end of our missions, that respect was fast turning into love for each other. We kept all the mission rules, but I did have an electrifying handshake.

Because the Korean War delayed our going on missions, we were both two years older than most returned missionaries when our missions concluded. Because of that, I felt the time to get married was now. Neither of us, as it used to be said, "had a red cent." Neither of us came from a family who could help us out financially. We were quite on our own when it came to matters of money. We had no car. We had no apartment. We had no prospects for things to get better. All we had was love and we felt we had more of that than any other couple had ever had. We felt that by being together we could do better in building the kingdom of God than we ever could alone.

We could have waited to get married. In a year we could have been a little better prepared. But to wait was the last option we considered. It never even occurred to us to wait. Looking back, we both know how foolish we were. Looking back, we both know how wise we were.

We were a couple who were a little like the brother of Jared and his wife—Sister Brother of Jared. The Lord touched the stones and gave them light to cross the great sea. In a sense, we said to the Lord, "Remember those stones you touched for the Jareds?" Could you reach down and touch our marriage and make it light up? Would you help our marriage and our family life to be bright and glorious?" From that time to this day, the Lord did indeed answer our prayers. He did reach down and place His finger into our lives each day to light up our marriage and family.

When I talk about our family being blessed, I'm not talking

about how others saw us. To them we were probably a dismal sight. But to us, who were part of the family, we were really something. Oh, the kids complained a lot and that sort of thing. However, somehow we all felt like we were quite a family. We were a little like the story of the enchanted cottage. Neither one of that couple in that cottage were very attractive to those who saw them. However, to each other they were beautiful.

Our Marriage

We were married in the Salt Lake Temple in 1956. At the conclusion of the reception that was held in that same city, when most of the people had departed, we sang many hymns with a few of our dearest friends who lingered with love. It seemed then and always that the best way to have the attitude of kingdom-building was to sing the songs of Zion and of the Savior.

Marilyn and I knew we could not have an extravagant honeymoon. However, we desired to have one anyway. So, after every one had departed, we drove in the car, that we had borrowed from my brother, five miles to Murray. There we got a room in a little motel by a little pond where we spent the night. They later tore that motel down, or maybe it fell down. I'm not sure. The next day, our glorious honeymoon was over and we drove to Provo.

Bearing our Testimonies to Each Other

Before our marriage, while on our missions, Marilyn with her missionary companion and I with mine, would bear our testimonies to our companions each morning just before prayer. I found then and now and always, that bearing one's testimony leads to an attitude of kingdom-building. Thus, Marilyn and I decided to continue to do that. Every morning we would each bear our testimony to the other. We had a gospel dream that defies description. We loved the Lord with great spiritual passion. We were not perfect, but we longed to be.

A Call to Serve

A month later, in our first ward, we were asked to be joint Sunday school teachers. We could not believe it! Someone like us being called to be teachers of others who were far more qualified than ourselves. I know it sounds a bit odd, but we felt the joy of that calling far more than any other calling we have ever received.

I could go on about these things. Not about how great we were in those days, but rather about how thrilled we were. Everything about the Church thrilled us. We could not get enough of it.

The thrill for us has never ended. We longed to serve. We longed to be part of this marvelous gospel. We longed to be spiritually right. We have struggled, we have wondered, but we have never faltered.

Seeking first the kingdom of God is not something that we can do because we know that we ought to. It is something, that because of inward feelings, we just can't help doing. It can only come if we are thrilled with the gospel. It can only happen if our hearts are set so much on the kingdom that it puts all else in the world way back on the stove of life. We cannot abandon the materialistic aspects of life. However, we can forever keep such matters in their place, as a secondary, rather than primary, parts of our dream.

How Can We Gauge How Well We Are Doing?

It is hard to always seek the kingdom of God first. Some days it seems we do it, and others days we do not. But there is a general direction, and we almost always know if we are deviating from the direction that leads to the kingdom of God. And if you never doubt that you are on your way to glory, then you are likely not on your way there at all. To assume that others are headed toward hell while we are coming closer each day to heaven is a sure sign that we have the first ticket to that lower place in our own pocket.

You have to feel like you don't quite measure up. However, that thought is among your greatest emotional pains. You have to wish with all your heart that you were able to do and feel the things that would insure that you were seeking the kingdom first.

Such feelings will lead you to pray and want to be close to the Savior, close to the Holy Ghost, close to our Heavenly Father. If such emotions are your greatest longing, then that, more than anything else, will be the sign that you truly desire to seek the kingdom of God first.

We All Can Do It

We are not talking about perfection here. We will all sin and come short of the glory of God. However, we are talking about having a perfect desire. To me the word "desire" will have more to do with our permanent membership in the Kingdom of God than any other word or feeling.

The best thing about seeking the kingdom of God first is that we can do it. I can do it. Marilyn and I can do it. Our children can do it. You and your spouse and your children can do it. In the name of Jesus Christ, we can do it. He, Jesus Christ, is not just our Savior when we die. He is our Savior now. If we desire, He gives us the power that will enable us to seek and to find the Kingdom first.

If You Want It, Jesus Christ Will Make It So

And if at times we fail, and we surely will, He, our Savior, if we have a broken heart and a contrite spirit, will make up the difference from where we are to where we long to be.

You Gotta Have Fun Along The Way

All this is not a solemn, serious, never-smile deal. Instead, all of this is fun. If you are not having fun, you are seeking the wrong things first. If you are not having fun, no one will like you and they won't let you help them. But your fun must be the kind of fun that everybody loves. It must be the kind of fun that everybody wants to be part of—the kind of fun where no one gets hurt in his or her heart. The kind of fun wherein you never make light of sacred things, and the most sacred thing is another person. Another sacred thing is the power to express love with one's wife or husband and to create life. The world makes light of this power. You never will. The law of chastity must always stand guard to protect your family from the damage of broken trust.

Come To the Center of the Gospel

When you truly seek first the kingdom of God, the foremost blessing is that you will have a feeling that God has, in the past, and now and forever, will flood your lives with His love, and that the future will be glorious.

In writing your life's symphony, don't get too hung up on the individual notes. Forever live so as to be able to hear the melody—the sweet, exciting and beautiful music of the Kingdom of God. Go ever deeper into that eternal music. Remember, the richest blessings are in the center of the gospel. That is the way to seek the Kingdom of God first, last and always—continually move toward the center of the gospel.

You'll Know

So go for it! Invite Jesus Christ to help you have the desire—the inward feeling to do all that you can to seek first His kingdom. Then listen to the heavenly music of the Holy Ghost and follow your heart into your glorious future. In your better moments you will always know that you are on the right path.

To all this you will likely say, "Amen." However, you would likely add, "I think I understand what you are saying. But I have a question. You say that by seeking first the kingdom of God, you will receive all these things. What are all these things? Are they money and fame or what?"

I reply, "I will try to explain. Read on."

CHAPTER 5

What Are All These Things That Are Promised?

The best answer I can give to your question, "What are all these things?" is to speak to you from my heart about what they are to me.

An Example Of All These Things

Perhaps I can more fully explain what all these things are by telling of an experience I had many years ago when our eight children were all still at home.

Our family had a tradition of eating scones on some wonderful evenings. One Sunday night I had a yearning for scones. I asked Marilyn, "Could you make some scones tonight if I would help?"

She replied, "It is so much work to make scones and I'm so tired."

"I know," I said sympathetically. "I figured it out and the work involved in making these delicious morsels just barely comes within the limits of what one should do on the Sabbath Day."

She softened and replied, "If you would help, and see that things get cleaned up afterward, I guess I could do it."

I was overjoyed.

Soon the bread dough was cut into pieces about the size of a dollar bill. In a few minutes the first half-dozen pieces of white dough sizzling in the hot oil had turned into light brown scones.

Marilyn placed these delicious treats in a large pan in the center of our round table. The other nine of us surrounded them with great glee, ready to pounce.

Before we began the feast I asked for silence and said, "Now it is time for our prayer. I will call upon our most outstanding family member to lead us in prayer." I looked at each family member while all waited for me to call on the chosen one. Finally I said, "I will call on the best-looking, the most popular, and the most intelligent family member." I added, "I will call on the one that we all love and admire." By this time each of the eight children spoke up and said, "I gave the prayer last time."

Then after a pause, wherein I considered which one most needed, at that time, to be honored, I called on him or her. The others groaned and moaned and complained, with good nature, that the one I had chosen did not fit the description I had given. The one chosen would look around with some degree of pride. All this was done in great humor and the family members loved this ritual. I saw to it that each one had his or her turn at being the honored one to give our sacred prayer.

Then after the "amen" we eagerly began to eat. As we did so, Marilyn returned to the stove to cook more scones so that we could have them while they were hot. As we ate I would tell jokes and say many humorous things. At least I thought that they were humorous. I told one joke that I made up. I like to make up jokes. I asked, "What would you have if a man named Richard carved a boat out of a potato?" None knew the answer. I replied with an all-knowing tone, "You would have a Dick tater ship."

They all booed and told me that I had told a dumb joke. They always did that. I could tell wonderful jokes and they would not laugh. Marilyn would then tell a joke that was not nearly the quality of mine, and they would laugh long and loud. They did that to persecute me.

Before going on, I must interject the fact that after dinner they would go to the phone and tell their friends the jokes I had told them. They would thus become popular with their friends because of the quality of these jokes. Meanwhile, back at the table as we continued to eat, I would say, "Please pass the butter."

Marilyn would say. "It is margarine, not butter."

I would reply, "I know that." But I would still call it butter because that made it taste better.

Marilyn would also fry eggs that were sunny side up. There is nothing more delicious than dipping a hot scone, dripping with butter, into an egg yoke and taking a big bite, and washing it down with a swallow of ice cold milk.

We would sit there and talk of all that was going on at school, and at church, and in the world of sports, and all sorts of serious and humorous matters. We would discuss, and laugh, and praise and eat, and laugh, and eat some more.

Then it was almost as if I could hear a knocking on the window. It was as if I opened the window so many blessings would pour in that they would cover our whole family completely over our heads in blessing "with all these things" that have been promised.

In this story "all these things" was not the house (although that was one of them). Nor was, "all these things" the table and chairs upon which we sat. Nor was "all these things" the stove, nor the pans, nor the butter, nor the eggs, nor the milk, nor even the magnificent scones.

Instead, "all these things" were the feelings we each felt in our hearts—the feelings of love, the feelings of security, the feelings of goodwill, the feelings of faith, the feelings of being together, the feelings that are too precious and deep to ever be described. "All these things" are the feelings that can only come from a Father in Heaven who has so many blessings for us who long for such blessings and who live for such blessings, that we can not fully contain them.

Conclusion

For us to have added to us "all these things" would be a blessing beyond measure and beyond description. And to have our children have added to them, "all these things' would be a most exalted joy. The realization of this family dream of receiving "all these things" would indeed be the makings of a glorious present and a glorious future.

It is in seeking the kingdom of God first that we have the greatest guarantee that not only us, but all our children, will indeed receive "all these magnificent spiritual blessings."

You reply, "I'd like those kinds of good-feeling things in my life. But how about money and material things? Are these things also part of all these things?"

I answer, "In a way they are. Let me explain. Read on."

CHAPTER 6

Woes, Worries, And Wonders

I have a response to your question, "How about money and material things? Are they part of "all these things"?

I say that the promise of the Lord goes far beyond money. The more part of the promise centers on those things that money cannot buy. However, money is, as you know first hand, a vital matter in our lives. It is a matter in which we all share a deep interest. So, as an example of life's challenges that sometimes seems to thwart a glorious future, let's talk about money, or the lack thereof.

Let's not talk about budgeting, spending less than you earn, getting rid of almost all of your credit cards, staying out of debt, or selling real-estate on the side.

Those things have already been said in a far better way than I could say them.

This book is about the boldest financial promise ever made: "Seek ye first the kingdom of God, and his righteousness; and all these things shall be added unto you." (Matt 6:33)

It is that promise which is the key to all financial matters.

We Will Still Have Woes

I almost said that promise would end all financial woes. However, perfectly applying God's great promise will not bring an end to our financial woes. We need "woes" or life would not be what it is supposed to be—what it needs to be. A life without woes would be like a football game without foes. It wouldn't make sense.

I sometimes think money's main purpose is to help us deal with the stress and worry that comes to each of us as we look forward, even into the immediate future, and ask ourselves, "How can we possibly make ends meet?"

Stress and worry about money helps us to gain the exercise we need to be able to deal with matters far more important than money. So go ahead and be stressed about money or the lack thereof. Such stress is good for you if you know it is paired with the knowledge that things have worked out in the past and they will in the future. That is the Lord's great promise.

Marilyn and I have never had enough money. I mean not even enough for the non-luxury items. We could not afford a good car, and so our car would almost spitefully break down and we would have to give up almost all else to get it fixed. Perhaps I should not discuss these personal matters. Yet, they are true for us, and I feel they might, to a greater or lesser degree, be true for you.

There were so many times when it was obvious that we would not make it financially for the next month or even the next week. But, the miracle is that we did. Don't ask me how we did. I don't know. The only thing I do know is the boldest promise ever made to us, and that is, "George and Marilyn, if you will seek my kingdom first, I will give you all the things you need. You still need to worry and fret and do all you can. But in the end, if you seek Me first and pay your tithing, I will miraculously give you all these things that you need."

It Is In Looking Back That We Really See

So many blessings are only seen by looking back. Marilyn and I often shake our heads in disbelief as we look back at where we once were and how we made it through. That is why we would like to see businesses give a discount not to us seniors, but to those juniors who are now in the midst of supporting a young family and who wonder almost every day, "How can we make ends meet?"

You younger families who have a difficult time just paying the bills for things like heat and lights, medical costs, a modest home, and an unimpressive car, to you who have to sacrifice greatly to give your children piano lessons, basketball shoes, and other things that just seem to be a bit more than you can afford, I say, "Because you sought first the kingdom of God, you will find out someday that ends did meet and the ends were beautiful. It will take woes and worries, but the wonders and miracles will come—including just barely enough money."

The Family Blessings of Not Having Much Money

There will be times when you will think that it is not happening. However, as the years pass, you will see that it has happened. Someday you will look back and in amazement wonder, "How did it happen?" Then you will realize that you have, miraculously, had a glorious financial past as well as a glorious financial future.

Of course you will have to budget. Of course you will have to skimp and make do. Of course you will have to look for sales. Of course you will have to cut coupons. Of course your older children will have to get jobs to support themselves and others in the family. Of course you will have to cut your own lawn, and do your own house work.

Of course you will have to have less distant vacations. Of course father will not be able to have expensive hobbies. Of course you won't have the latest clothes and house décor unless you have the thrill of doing it yourself. Of course your home will not be awesomely large. Of course you will have to pray for your car to start on cold mornings.

But remember this—not having excess money is the best way to raise children. When you do not have much money, that gives you the liberty, and even the necessity, of saying "no" to many of their requests.

However, you need to say "no" with a smile on your face as you add, "No, you can't have a snowmobile. But when we get rich we will each have one of the best snowmobiles ever made." Your children will then turn away while saying, "Sure, Mom and Dad. Sure."

Knowing You Are on the Right Path

On the other hand, when you are doing all you can to support the children in love and encouragement, when you are serving in the Church, when you are having family prayer, paying your tithes and offerings, when you are having family home evening, when you are doing things together as a family, and loving each other, and when you know that you are not perfect, but wish you could be. Then you will quietly, surely, and miraculously receive "all these things."

So look ahead. What do you see? I don't mean down at your feet. Look up in the sky. Yes indeed, you have a glorious future. The Lord has promised you that.

The Miracles of Making Ends Meet

I feel that I can speak with some authority on these matters because of the experiences Marilyn and I have had though the years. Here is a brief sketch of the things—the miracles—that have happened to us.

A Place to Live

The man who the Lord used to set up this miracle was Oscar Mink. He was an enterprising graduate student at BYU. He and his wife, Julia, had bought an old house near campus. A few months before Marilyn and I married, Oscar and Julia were inspired to build a little "lean-to" apartment on the back of their old house. I don't think today's building codes would have allowed such a little unit. But they built it. I'm sure the reason the Lord had them do so was because in just a few months, Marilyn and I would get married, and would need a place to live. So just as the last nail was driven and the place was ready, we were searching for a place to live.

Marilyn saw a listing for this little apartment in the BYU housing office. She went to the listed address and rented the place the Lord had built for us. Miraculously it was so little that it only cost us $45 per month. That was just $45 more than our zero income. No other place in Provo was so reasonable.

We moved in on a muddy, rainy, January night. Inside it was warm and cozy. We were so happy there. That place was full of "all these things." I mean, I don't think anyone was ever as happy anywhere as we were there. It was a glorious chapter in our lives.

A Job for Marilyn

The next morning, after we moved into our little bit of heaven, Marilyn went to the offices of the phone company in Provo. She had worked for this company in Salt Lake City. However, when she asked about transferring to Provo, they told her there were no openings in Provo. The day after our arrival in Provo, she was prompted to try anyway. That morning, a lady at the phone company in Provo was miraculously inspired to leave her job at the telephone company. Just as this lady walked out the door, Marilyn walked in. Five minutes later, the lady's former job was Marilyn's.

My mother and father gave us food. Things like potatoes and such. It is amazing how far that food went. BYU used to show movies. Admittance was 25 cents. We could afford that once each week. We just had to skip the popcorn. We had no car, but there was not any place we needed to go that we could not walk. I'm not saying any of this to make you feel sorry for us. I am just trying to make you jealous.

Being Able to Afford a Baby

The best news I have ever received was the news that Marilyn gave me when she said, "We are going to have a baby." However, with this good news came an attached worry. We wondered how we could pay for the birth of the baby with no insurance or other means. The Lord then miraculously arranged with the U.S.

Government for me to be drafted into the Army. I think He was growing weary of having to do things for us. So He felt the Army would solve our problems for the next two years. That way He could concentrate on the other more needy people.

The Army was great. They gave me housing. They gave me food. They gave a few dollars for me and a few for Marilyn. And best of all, they had a hospital where Marilyn went and had *our five-dollar baby*, Matthew Burnham Durrant. As Matt has grown up I have often told him, "Matt, you cost us five dollars, but you have been worth it." He has appreciated that. I think.

Our First Car

The army sent me to Korea. During the time I was there, we saved $50 dollars a month. We were fast becoming rich. A year and a half later, when I came out of the Army, we rode the bus to Salt Lake City and bought an eight-year-old 1950 Chevrolet. We felt we could see the USA in our Chevrolet. As we drove home, we were so thrilled. It was not an attractive car. So I spent the next week polishing the fenders, hood, top and trunk. Soon the black paint came alive and glistened with the one-fourth inch covering of simonize wax. I noticed people were looking at the car with envy as I drove down the highway. I love it when people think that I am rich. That old car was a beauty.

My First Job

When I was about to be discharged from the Army, I think the Lord might have said, "Oh, no! George will soon be back." In preparation for that time, He had the BYU officials build five giant men's residence buildings called Helaman Halls.

They were ready for occupancy just as I arrived back at BYU for my final year of school. I interviewed to be one of the head residents. There were many applications—most of them were far more impressive than mine. I have never interviewed well if I really wanted the job. In my interview for that job, the boss was not impressed. However, I noticed that he was working on some posters. I was a bit of an artist, so I asked if I could give him a hand. We worked together for a few days on the posters and he started to like me. So he hired me to be the head resident at David John Hall. That gave Marilyn, little Matthew, and me a little apartment, a little money, and all the food we could eat.

A Profession

I was about to graduate from college. Now what? We needed another miracle.

I wanted to become a school teacher. I considered going to California to teach. That was where the big bucks were. But then a lady told me she thought I looked and acted like a seminary teacher. I was flattered by that. Besides, I had seen young men do many sad things while I served in the Army in Korea. What I had seen made me realize there was a great need to teach the youth so that they could withstand the temptations out in the world. So I decided, with the blessings of Marilyn, that being a seminary teacher was what I wanted to become. I decided to get information on what I would have to do to be part of that profession.

I went to the office of the seminary officials. I had been told to see a certain man who hired new teachers. When I arrived, the man I wanted to see was not there. I was disappointed because this man was really flamboyant, and I felt he was the one who would give me the best chance of getting a job that many others wanted.

Looking back, I now know that it was the Lord who had miraculously had him step out of his office for an hour or so. His assistant was available. The secretary told me that I could see this other man. I hesitated, but I had no choice. This assistant was a quiet, sincere man who listened more than he talked. Somehow I was not afraid of him as I would have been with the other man. After I told this man of my desires, and why I wanted to teach seminary, he told me that he had a feeling I would be a good teacher. His words encouraged me. I needed to be encouraged, for I did not have great confidence in myself.

This man made an appointment for me to see a higher official of the seminary system. I didn't do well in that interview. As I left the interview I had little hope of ever getting a job. An hour or so after that interview, in Brigham City, Utah, a seminary teacher miraculously decided to leave his position at the local seminary. I feel the Lord had him leave so that I could come.

When the official with whom I had just been interviewed learned that this position was open, he thought of me. Why did he think of me? I had interviewed so poorly. I feel that it was the Lord who caused him to think of me. It is always more important to impress the Lord than to impress anyone else. This official called me in and asked if I was willing to go wherever I was asked. I told him that I was. He then told me that he wanted me to go to Brigham City. I could not believe it. I loved the tree-lined streets of Brigham City. I felt like all this was just too big of a miracle, and must just be a dream. However, it was not just a dream, and soon we were headed to Brigham City.

Upon arriving there, we sadly learned that Brigham City was in the midst of a building boom. Thiokol had just been built and many workers moved there to work in the rocket industry. Houses were scarce and too expensive for us. However, there was a contractor there who the Lord used as an instrument to miraculously help us out. This man had a little plot of land—far too small to build a house on. He went to the planning commission and they knew a little house would soon be needed for George and Marilyn and their growing little family. Well, they did not know it, but the Lord did. So they bent the rules and told the man he could build a little house there.

Just as the little house was complete, Marilyn and I drove into town. We were led to the little house. It was just barely within our ability to pay. Well, it was really a little more than we could pay. All of our houses have been a little bit more than we could pay. However, the Lord always helped us, if we would sacrifice, to just barely make it.

We loved our time in Brigham City. The seminary officials wanted me to help with the Indian Seminary, which was then at the Intermountain Indian School. He loved the Indians and felt I could succeed with them.

Working with the Indians changed my life. Marilyn and I became part of the great promise that was made to the people of Brigham City by the Prophet George Albert Smith. At a meeting in the historic tabernacle a few months before the Indian school began to operate, this prophet told the large assembly of people that whoever of them would set his or her hand and heart to help the Indian young people who would soon come to their city, they would receive blessings beyond measure.

It was sort of one of those "seek the kingdom first and you shall receive all else" sort of promises. Those promised blessings really happened for us.

I loved the young Indian students. I loved them beyond my ability to say. I became the principal of the Indian Seminary and the branch president to all the Indian adults and their families who worked at the school.

A Thanksgiving Turkey

I recall my first Thanksgiving in Brigham City. I went home for lunch and as I drove along, I was listening to KSL radio. A cooking expert named Margaret Masters was talking about how to cook a Thanksgiving turkey. I felt sad because I knew we would not have a turkey. I longed for a turkey. I longed to be rich.

When I got back to the regular seminary where I taught a few classes, the principal, LeGrande Horsely, handed me a big box. He said, "The seminary central office has sent us each a turkey and here is yours." I almost heard the Lord say, "Here is your turkey, but don't get the idea that you will be rich." I could hardly teach my next class because of the gratitude that I felt.

A Christmas Bike

A few weeks later, Christmas was nearly upon us. Our oldest son, Matt, wanted a new bike for Christmas. It was beyond our income. Then, out of the blue, an Indian man named Chris Windchief called on the phone and said, "I was thinking about you for some reason. My son, Sweeny Windchief, has a bike that he does not ride any more. Could you use anything like that?"

I hurried down to get it. My eyes filled with tears as I considered why this man had called me. I painted the bike a bright red and it looked new. My son Matt was so glad to get the bike on that memorable Christmas morning.

A Christmas Tree

That was the same Christmas when all the seven Seminary teachers in Brigham City went up into the mountains to harvest our own Christmas trees. I took my young son, Matt. Soon we were in deep snow, and Matt and I were not equipped for that. We just had on our shoes. We did not own any boots. We excused ourselves from the expedition and headed home. I began to feel sorry for myself, wishing I could afford better clothes and things. I wished that I had a Christmas tree. I wished I could be rich.

That night, about nine o'clock, the seminary teachers all came to our house. They said, "We want you to have the best tree that we found." It was a beauty. They left the house and I tearfully put the tree in place. I almost heard the Lord say, "Well, here is your tree. However, don't expect to become rich." I'll love those men—those seminary teachers—forever for many reasons, but mostly because of that tree. With friends like them, I didn't have to be rich.

I could go on and on about these specific miracles that came to us. It was like that all along the way though the years.

Always Just in Time

Miracles did not come a year or month or even a week in advance. They didn't come until almost all the worrying and the tears were used up. They just came exactly when it seemed that we could not make it.

They came, and suddenly our dismal looking future became glorious. Miracles seem to be more treasured when they come so late that you know they are not just coincidences.

Other Kinds Of Miracles

As I write this, I now chuckle over our financial struggles. However in the past, there were plenty of times we did not chuckle. We knew the stress that came from the lack of money.

The Miracle of a Sense of Humor

Incidentally, if you don't have the money to live the high life, you can salve the supposed pain with a sense of humor. Marilyn and I often joke that when her parents first saw our little engagement diamond, her mother said, "At least our daughter is not marrying a spendthrift." And her father said, "You don't often see a diamond like that. The light has to be just right."

To make it financially on a meager income, you have to have a sense of humor. You have to laugh at your woes or you will spend your whole time crying. I feel our Heavenly Father gave us the miracle of a sense of humor to soften the pains and anxieties of trying to make ends meet.

The Miracle of Strength

Sometimes you just can't laugh off your woes, however. There is a time to laugh and a time to cry. I think Heavenly Father does not like to see us cry. So when He sees our tears and hears our prayers He sends us a miracle. He always does that. His miracles often can't be seen except by looking back. Often His greatest miracle is the gift of strength—the strength to make it though narrow and hard places.

With the miracles of inspired understanding, and a sense of

humor mixed with tears, and with the strength that can always come when we seek it through prayer, we are ready to constantly find our glorious future.

The Miracle of Opportunity

Other miracles can be those of opportunity. I loved teaching the Indian students, but the regular Church curriculum did not seem to apply to them. So I began to write our own lessons.

This opened the door to my writing career. Many years earlier, my mother had supported me in college. I majored in art, and buying my supplies cost her much money.

She told me one day, "George, I don't mind helping you get the paper and paints so you can create these pictures, however, your greatest pictures will not be painted with these things. Your greatest pictures will be painted with your words. Your pen, not your brush, will be where you will paint pictures that will be a great blessing to others."

I had no idea what she meant, but the Lord did. That is one of the reasons He sent me to Brigham City. That is what that man meant who interviewed me to be a seminary teacher when he told me I would perform miracles in the seminary program.

Soon I was called into the seminary offices at Brigham Young University to write lessons for the Indians. Because of what I was doing in the Indian Curriculum, I was asked to be part of the committee that would write the first Family Home Evening lessons for the Church. When I was called to that important committee, I went to a meeting conducted by Elder Harold B. Lee.

Up until that time everyone who received a calling to the general Church committees were announced with their picture in the *Church News*. I really looked forward to that because I had never had my picture in any newspaper, let alone the *Church News*. Then Elder Lee announced that day, "We have decided that those called to Church committees will no longer have their pictures in the *Church News*."

I have to admit I was quite disappointed.

After the meeting, an older man named Reid Bradford—one of the great ones who always sought the kingdom of God first, and who had truly received all else—came to me. He said, "George, isn't it wonderful that you will get to do all this work in secret. Then the Lord will be able to bless you openly."

The Lord prompted Brother Bradford to tell me that. It meant so much to me then and now.

I learned many things on that committee from people who sought the kingdom first. They taught me so much about how to raise my young family. My experience on the committee added yeast to my life that truly leavened the whole loaf of my life.

But none of "these things" brought me more money. We still struggled to pay our bills. "These things" just brought me satisfaction and joy and wisdom on how to relate to Marilyn and to the children.

The success of the lessons I wrote for the Indians led to my being called to come to Salt Lake City to work there on Family Home Evening and Priesthood Home Teaching programs for the entire Church.

We bought a house in Salt Lake City that had crooked walls. That irregular and highly imperfect structure made it so we could afford it. After a while, the crooked walls seemed straight and charming to us. We put up inexpensive shutters and painted our front door. It looked a bit Cape Codish. We imagined we lived in New England.

After reading all this, you reply, "Wow! I love those miracles. But I'd like to have more money than you and Marilyn have had. How do I do that?"

I reply with great understanding, "I don't blame you for wanting more money than we had. How much money do you want? If that is what you desire, that is probably what you will get. Read on."

CHAPTER 7

If You Desire Much Money As Part Of "All These Things," You May Receive It

You asked about making money. Here is my best shot at answering that. The Lord through the prophet Jacob taught the Nephites:

"But before ye seek for riches, seek ye first the kingdom of God.

"And after ye have obtained a hope in Christ ye shall obtain riches, if ye seek them for the intent to do good." (Jacob 2:18-19)

You Will Get Just What You Desire

One of the most powerful words in religion is the word *"desire."* What do you really desire? Whatever you truly desire is exactly what you will get. That does not mean that if you desire to be the most prominent person in your profession that it will come to pass. If you have the right set of talents and if you pursue your work with all your heart you might become just what you desire. However, you might ultimately fall short of that desire. This is true in all aspects of life where you are comparing your success to the success of others and measuring your success by that data.

On the other hand, if you desire to be the best you can possibly be in your profession, and if you seek the kingdom of God first, then that will happen and you will excel. These are desires that you can attain and all those around you can also attain. There is no competition on achieving such desires. These sorts of desires are centered in things related to all matters concerning inward self-improvement and service to your fellow men. If you desire these things with all your heart, and as you seek the kingdom of God first, then you will indeed achieve them.

Want With All Your Heart to Build the Kingdom of God

We can succeed in any righteous field or endeavor if we truly desire to seek the kingdom of God first, and if our desires are to serve Him continually in righteousness.

A friend told me this story about himself:

Many years ago, when I was a struggling college student, I met the girl of my dreams. I fell in love with her and she with me. We decided that we would like to get married. At the time, I had no great prospects to gain many of the things of the world.

I made an appointment to talk to her father about the matter of marriage. After exchanging some pleasantries about the weather and so on I girded up my loins, took a deep breath, and announced to the rather austere man that I desired to marry his daughter.

The father's expression became stern as he asked, "How do you propose to support her?"

I hemmed and hawed a bit about how I planned to become a teacher and that I was sure that somehow I could provide for her financial needs. The father who had accumulated many of this world's goods was not impressed with the future prospects for his beloved daughter.

Sensing I was not winning the favor of the father, I sat up straight in my chair and announced in a firm and convincing manner, "Sir, I do not have much money now, and perhaps I never will. However, I'll tell you one thing for certain. I'll guarantee you right here and now that I will take your daughter all the way to the celestial kingdom."

This powerful statement sank deep into the father's heart. After a pause he said, "That is good enough for me. You have my permission to marry my daughter. That which you have so boldly announced you will do for her is what I really want for my daughter."

This fellow's answer reveals that his primary goal was to seek first the kingdom of God. Did he later make a whole bunch of money? No, he did not. But others, whom I have known, who were centered in the kingdom did indeed make much money. So you never know. I hope you do make a lot of money. I know you will use it to do good.

Things Will Work Out

But a far greater promise than that of wealth untold is the promise that things will work out.

When a couple marries, and each desires more than anything else to someday be worthy to enter the kingdom of God, then that is really all that matters. Oh, sure you have to earn a living and all those sorts of things! But those things will work out if you desire to someday make it to the kingdom of God, and if you live each day in such a way that you are already in the kingdom of God.

Problems, yes, you'll have those. Disagreements with each other, oh, sure, you will have those. Money shortages, you bet you'll have those. Disappointments, you'll have plenty of those. Heartbreaks, of course you'll have those. However, your heartbreaks will be uninvited heartbreaks, and not the kind that your behavior invites into your lives.

If you are looking up to that high mountain called the "kingdom of God," and you seek that above all else, then you can make it through all the dark and difficult valleys, rocks, weeds, and crevasses of the present. You'll see meaning in every difficulty, and you will always have direction.

I'm not talking about perfection. You won't be perfect. Your marriage won't be perfect. Your children won't be perfect. However, your desire will be perfect. And that is all that ultimately matters. Other things will seem to matter, and they really will for a time. But in the long run, you will reach your greatest desire—the kingdom of God. You will indeed, according to your desire, have "all these things added to you." You will have a glorious future.

After reading this chapter, you ask, "What comes first, the kingdom of God or the family?"

I reply, "Great question! Read on."

CHAPTER 8

The Family And The Kingdom Of God

You asked about the relationship between the family and the kingdom of God. The relationship is: they are to one and the same. Never is it one or the other; it is always both.

Jon Huntsman, Jr., is currently the governor of the state of Utah. When I see him on TV or read of him in the newspaper I place much trust in him. I feel he is a very good man. I mention this because his father is a rich man. The senior Huntsman must have great satisfaction in what he has personally accomplished in his life. He has built a renowned industrial kingdom in the world. Yet in his heart, I'm sure that the senior Huntsman's greatest source of inward satisfaction comes as he and his wife observe the successes of their children, and in this case, their son's success as an honorable leader of men, as a loving husband, and as a devoted father.

Satisfaction is in the Family

Many years ago our family lived on the edge of a fairly affluent area of Salt Lake City. We attended church with people who were highly successful financially. These folks, though humble in their approach to life, took some satisfaction in the fact that they were successful.

They would have rather lavish wedding receptions when one of their children married. They loved their drapes, their carpets and fine cars. Some longed to move even further up the hill where the bigger homes were.

When mingling with the women of these households and when the latest fashions and the exclusive home decorations were discussed in informal gatherings, Marilyn—my wife—remained silent. Once after a meeting of the women who served in the Relief Society Presidency, Marilyn rode home with one of the leaders.

This lady said, "I noticed when we were all discussing having our homes redecorated that you were silent."

Marilyn replied, "We can't afford to have our home redecorated, so I had nothing to say."

Her friend replied, "We all take a good deal of pride in our fashion and in having the latest to wear and to live in. We like to have just a bit bigger wedding reception than the last one we attended. It is our way of saying that we are successful. It is part of our feelings of self-worth."

Marilyn did not reply.

The other woman said, "We have all watched you and your family closely since you moved into our area. You don't care about things like that, do you?"

"Oh, sure I do. It's just that it isn't that important to me," Marilyn replied.

The woman then said, "You don't seem to feel a need to have to prove yourself with things like that. Your children and your family life give you the satisfaction that we all seek in displaying our evidences of wealth. Your self-worth comes from your home, not your house."

Marilyn smiled and thanked her for the second-hand clothes she had recently brought to our son, beautiful clothes that her son had outgrown. We will never forget the chapter of our lives wherein we lived among these choice people.

I don't relate this story to make any claim that our family is any better or even as good as the other families in that area. It's just that we really haven't ever felt any need to keep up with the Joneses or any other family when it comes to "all *those* things." That is in part due to the fact that we just never had the funds to keep up with anybody. We sometimes wished that we did have such money. However, we did not and still don't.

Those families we just mentioned were remarkable in our eyes. We loved them. They were so generous to us. They would take our children in their boats and on special outings. It was then that we learned that it is better to have a neighbor who has a boat than it is to have a boat ourselves. Many of these folks were heroes to our children. Their children were deeply talented and good. It is just that we are not talking about them. We are talking about our family.

This part of the book is not about other families, it is only about your family, about my family. Not how your family compares to other families, but only how your family compares to themselves. It is not a matter of money, how much or how little you have. It is a matter of what comes first to you: the kingdom of the world or the kingdom of God.

What Really Matters?

A famous man, a member of the Church of Jesus Christ of Latter-day Saints, was very wealthy. He became involved in horse racing. He had many horses of his own. He dreamed of someday having a horse capable of winning the Kentucky Derby, the Preakness, and the Belmont Stakes—the Triple Crown. Finally, he had such a horse.

This famous horse was, at that time, one of the two most notable horses in the world. This horse had won many races and was destined to win many more. This horse could possibly be one of the greatest racers of all time. This man had a family who also rejoiced in the horse as much as the father did.

One day, while at his office, a dear friend phoned him and in a solemn tone said, "I'm afraid I have some terrible news for you."

The rich man automatically jumped to the most dreadful

conclusion he could imagine and he replied, "Something has happened to my horse."

It turned out that the bad news was not related to the horse or the family. It was the failure of a business deal. The man, hearing what it was, felt relieved. In the next hour or two he considered the phone call and of his thought that to him the saddest news he could ever receive was that something had happened to his horse. He lamented that he hadn't first thought that the saddest news he could hear was that something had happened to his wife or to one of his children. Instead it was that something had happened to his horse.

This served as a wake-up call to this man. He began from that time forth to rearrange his priorities. He desired with all his heart to think first of his family and in a sense to think first of the kingdom of God.

A Heartfelt Point of View

It all seems to come down to a point of view—a point of view that comes not from the eyes but from the heart. On what do you set your heart? Is it drapes and receptions and furnishings? Is it set on success in your career? Or is it set on honor and service and the family? Oh, sure, there is a time to think of gaining the comfort that comes from a fine home and other of this world's possessions, but first must come the kingdom. The kingdom of God must always be the horse, and then "all these things" will be the carriage. You must make certain you don't get the carriage (all these things) before the horse (seek first the kingdom of God).

The Couple and the Children

On a related note, we are all different as to how many children we could or should have. Never should we relate the size of a family (the number of children) to the quality of the family. However, if you can, even at considerable sacrifice, have all the children that wisdom and your personal revelation will allow. This will aid you in seeking the kingdom first. So, when it comes to the number of children you are to have, this is the best counsel: "Do not stop having children until you have had your last one." The last one is always such a bonus. Parents do not know what they would have done without their last one—or the first one, or all the middle ones. To have children is a blessing that cannot be adequately described. Be your children naturally born or adopted, it is all the same. Both of these conditions are determined in a Higher Place.

Each child we have, or desire to have, is an added proof that we are seeking the kingdom of God first. I love the words of Jesus when he saw that those around him were shunning the children. He said, "Suffer the little children to come unto me for of such is the kingdom of God."

You reply to what you just read by saying, "I agree that the greatest contribution I can make to the kingdom of God is to have a good family. However, it seems to me that the greatest thing that parents can do for their children is to make sure they provide their children with opportunities and a good life. It takes dedication to one's work to make the money needed to provide these necessary things. And besides that I feel an inward need to succeed not only at home but also in my career. So my question is, 'How do I, or we, as parents, divide our time between our family and our work?'"

I reply, "I understand what you are asking. I've thought a lot about that. Read on."

CHAPTER 9

For Where Your Time Is Spent, There Will Your Heart Be Also

You asked, "How should I divide my time between my family and my work?" That is a great question, and one which that will be a struggle for a father, and sometimes for a mother, each day of your child rearing years. The way you live your answer to this question will have a great bearing on how well you, in the long run, seek first the kingdom of God.

Don't Halt Between Two Opinions

When Marilyn and I became parents, our way of "seeking first the kingdom of God" took a slight turn. We sort of gained a new set of eyes. Our time priorities changed. We began to long for our children to do well more than we desired ourselves to do so. However, I, as do most, often halt between two opinions. We do want our children to do well, but there is a continual pull that makes each of us want to do well ourselves. Often we mistakenly tell ourselves, "I dedicate myself and my time to success in my own work and career because if that success comes, I will be better able to help my children succeed."

A great man once asked me, "George, would you sooner be honored in the world or in the Church, or would you rather have your child receive such honor?" He did not expect me to answer. Then he added, "When you decide on how you would answer that question, then you will know all that really matters."

If personal satisfaction and so-called success continue to be our highest priority, then we are just exactly backward in our approach to the great commandment and blessing of seeking first the kingdom of God and all these things shall be added to us. We try to add these things first and then the kingdom. As I said before, we put the carriage before the horse.

However, and this is a big however, if we have as our first priority the well-being of our spouse and children, then often times, among the other things that will be added will be success in our work and other aspects of our personal and material life.

Marilyn and I always considered our family to be part and the heart of the kingdom of God.

No Other Success

Never have we had a busier time in our family life than we did when I served as mission president in the Kentucky/Tennessee Mission. I had a basic tenet that helped me keep my perspective at that hectic and demanding time. That tenet, simply stated was:

When the three years of this service ended I would not take any missionary or any convert or any program home with me. All I would take home with me would be Marilyn and the children. Therefore, while I served this mission, my family would come first and all else second.

The Visit of an Angel

I recall that soon after we arrived in Kentucky, a young newly married lady came to see me. She announced that she had a special message for me based upon her own experience. As I recall she said something like this.

"President Durrant, I feel by the Holy Spirit that I must give you a special message. A few years ago, I was a mission president's daughter and I still feel the pain of that experience. My father is a wonderful man and he was a wonderful mission president. However, during the time of our family service in the mission field, he was not a wonderful father. It seemed to me that everything other than the family came first, and then the family came next. He was almost always gone, and when he was home he really wasn't home at all."

Then she said rather sternly, "Some of your children are the same age that I was when we served. Don't put your children through what I went through. Center your life in them."

With that, she announced what she had come to say to me. She then rose and was gone. But what she said stayed with me. I feel that she was sent to me by the Lord to reinforce what I had already intended to do. At that time, and for the next three years, I fully realized how difficult this would be.

If the Family is First, Then All Else Will Be All Right

At the beginning of this mission our eight children ranged in age from fifteen down to one year. They were excited at the adventure of being in Kentucky, but they missed home, family, and friends. For some of them it was a very hard adjustment.

In the early days of my work in the mission, I was amazed at the demands that were thrust at me. I was tempted to give it my all—my time, my talent, and all that I had—thinking that, later, things would settle down and then I could have time for the family. Little did I know that things would never settle down. Two hundred missionaries were under my supervision and responsibility 24 hours each day, along with 100 cars, two states, and parts of three others, four mission districts, of which I was the president. Needless to say, these responsibilities could consume far more than 24 hours a day.

But Your Work Can Be So Exciting and Public Success So Appealing

And, oh, the joy of being out there among the missionaries and the saints and the meetings and the interviews and the phone calls! It was so appealing, so rewarding to be part of something so magnificent. I dreamed of being a good, and hopefully, a wonderful mission president. I knew that could only happen if I gave my heart completely to the glorious cause.

Now, looking back some thirty years, I thank the Lord that I sought first the kingdom of God and that all these other things were added to Marilyn and me. Somehow I held fast to my commitment to put the family first and that made all the difference. Our children loved the missionaries. Can you imagine the blessing of having your children know and love the noble young servants of the Lord? I used every opportunity to have the children mixed in with the missionaries.

The Swing: A Symbol of the Right Priorities

A week after we arrived in Louisville, I noticed a limb on the big tree in our front yard. In my mind, I could see a swing hanging from that limb. I went to the store and bought a long and strong rope. I called a couple of athletic elders over, and after I had prayer with them, I sent one of them up the tree. He bounded up like a monkey. Soon he was out on the limb. I was nervous. That tree was huge and the limb was really high. What would I tell his mother if he fell to the hard ground? Soon he had secured the rope and the other elder tied it to the seat. Then he secured the other end of the rope. Finally the elder was back on earth and the swing hung in its full majesty.

My oldest son was soon in the swing and the elders were pushing him so high I feared for airplanes flying over head. The other children shouted for a turn of their own. Neighbor children came from their houses. My children had instant friends.

The swing was the heart of our family recreation center and the symbol of my commitment to put the family first. We added a basketball court.

A month later, I attended a mission presidents' seminar in Atlanta. Elder S. Dilworth Young (one of the most beloved of all the past General Authorities) was the visiting authority. Toward the end of the first day of the conferences, each of the presidents was asked to take five minutes and describe some program he had implemented to move the work forward. Somehow, I was to be the last to give my report.

The others were wonderful leaders and their wise and powerful reports made me quake at what I could say that would in any way match what they had said. Some talked of tracting ideas, and others about ideas for zone conference. Another talked of how to motivate the missionaries to do great things and to baptize more than ever before. As exciting as these reports were, the hour of the day caused Elder Young to become a bit drowsy.

Finally, it was my turn. I arose and felt impressed to say, "The best thing I have done thus far on my mission is to build a swing." Everyone laughed. Elder Young, hearing the commotion, asked his marvelous wife, Hulda, "What did he say? What did he say?"

She replied, "He said that the best thing that he has done was to build a swing."

"A swing!" he said rather loudly.

I went on to explain the visit of the young lady and my desire to make my children happy and comfortable before launching out on other matters. Soon all were emotionally touched. Elder Young seemed to be deeply impressed. Through the following years he often reported the story of the mission president and the swing. The story became rather famous. Years have passed since then. The old tree is gone now, blown down by a windstorm several years after we came home. In my mind the tree still stands and the swing awaits my children, their friends, and any visitor, including General Authorities, who each had their turn on the swing.

The interesting thing was that in deciding to give my primary attention to my family, it became the foundation of my success as a mission president. The missionaries loved the Durrant children. They wanted them to come to everything. Of course they could not do that. But they could come often and they did. They could come to the Christmas zone conferences and come to many events in the summer when they were not in school. They could attend many closer events that did not require long travel. The missionaries liked to come to the mission home and see the family. They were interested in the successes of the children. They loved to hear me talk about family life and the importance of them as missionaries, doing well as missionaries being the best preparation for their future success as fathers and mothers and as spouses. The attention that I gave to the family took time away from the time I could give to the missionaries. However, it made the time I could give to the missionaries all the more effective. It was a true and vivid example of the validity of the Lords' promise that seeking the kingdom of God first would insure other successes.

I was not the most successful of all mission presidents. However I was the *greatest average* mission president the Church ever had, and my family recalls our mission experience as a grand and glorious time in their lives.

The Test Never Ends

The times before and after our mission were not without their trials in keeping the family first and foremost. I found, then and forever, that if you feel good about what is going on at home, you will be a much more effective employee at work. But, on the other hand, being the most successful employee and not having success at home can be a miserable way to live.

I have often said that any employee who leaves his employment will be almost immediately replaced by some employee who was glad to step in and fill the vacant position.

However, when a man or woman leaves his or her family, that mother or father can never be replaced. Surely, home is the place to give one's best effort.

But the work world is so demanding. You can let things slide at home. However, you cannot do that at work. If you don't do well at work, your family will suffer. If you do not get promoted, or even worse, lose your job, then things would really be difficult. The answer is to seek the kingdom of God first. If you do not do well at work, and if circumstances and people there are stacked against you, you can leave and all will be well. Sure, you will worry and there will be stress. But pretty soon, as you continue to seek the kingdom of God first, things will work out because you have the promise of a glorious future.

Dear Lord, Please Tilt Me Toward My Family

My beloved watercolor teacher, Carl Purcell, told our class this story:

Years ago there was a man who had two wives, one named Lillie and one named Tillie. He was always meticulously fair in the way that he treated them. If he purchased a new dress for Lillie, he did the same for Tillie. He was so very careful in all this.

Finally, Lillie died, and a year later, Tillie did the same. They were buried side by side with a space for him between. When he was near death, he told the mortician, "Be sure and bury me right in the center—equally close to both of them." But then with a twinkle in his eye he added, "But tilt me just a little bit toward Tillie."

You have to strike a balance between the effort you spend at work and the effort you make in assuring the well-being of your family. However, the balance must always be tilted slightly, or even more, in favor of the family.

Sometimes we are under financial demands, or the demands to make one's own business succeed, that we take a second job or spend endless hours in our fledgling business. Don't do it! I know you have to do what you feel you have to do, but remember, the thing you have to do is to be a good husband and father. Then all else will fall into place. Yes, it is a matter of faith. If you keep your priorities straight, then other things will work out—they just will.

But if you confuse your priorities, then nothing that matters will work out.

Even Church Work

Even church work can encroach upon family time. Sometimes we are called to a position in the Church and we long to do it well. If we are a bishop, we want to be a "hero bishop" who is everywhere. The people love such a bishop. They talk about him long after his release. They say he was in their home many times to counsel with them or their child. Let us hope that such a bishop was not the father of children. If so and if he is a "hero bishop," let us hope that his wife was extremely self-sufficient.

Be the kind of bishop who sends others into the homes. Be the kind of bishop who helps his people to be self-sufficient so that they do not need him for their every problem. Be a delegator. You may not want to do that. But you will likely pay the price if you do not.

Give me a bishop who is known best for his attention to his family, his attention to his wife, who is seeking the kingdom of God first at home and then in the ward. Of course such a bishop will be very involved in the work. He will do all that is necessary. However, he will not have his life's balance so tilted on the service side that his family will regret that he has been called as a bishop.

This is a matter of wisdom and of faith. It is a matter that requires much prayer. It is a matter that requires some difficult decisions. It is a matter wherein one must constantly remind oneself to seek the kingdom of God first, and to remember that the family is at the heart of the kingdom of God. It is a matter of seeking a glorious future. I recall this tough decision:

You Just Have to Decide

We were on our family mission. We love sports. We loved horse racing, but not the gambling. Horse racing is not made a sport by gambling, it is made a sport by the magnificent animals that look and run with the beauty of a god. Just to see these mighty thoroughbreds is a thrill. And to see them run is a miracle in motion—a deeply emotional experience.

The Kentucky Derby is run right there in Louisville where we lived. For a year we had planned to go, as a family, on the first Saturday in May to watch the three-year-olds thunder down the tract in their quest for "the roses."

One week before the big race, I received a call that the visiting General Authority to the Lexington Stake Conference had changed his time for that conference by one week and that it was now to be held on the first Saturday and Sunday in May. I had no responsibility at the conference other then to give a short talk on Sunday. However, the General Authority asked me to come on Saturday. So I had a decision. Would I go to the conference or to the Derby?

(What would you have done?)

I called the Authority and told him of my dilemma. He answered, "Sometimes we just have to choose."

So it was up to me. I could not disappoint the children, and so we went to the Derby on Saturday and the next day attended the Sunday portion of the stake conference. When I saw the visiting authority, he just smiled. I don't know what he thought of me. However, I knew what I thought of me. I felt a bit guilty. I often feel that way. Many years have passed and I can't remember much about that stake conference, however I can remember standing there near the fence, with my family, on the infield of Churchill Downs and watching the great horse Secretariat thunder by. I never missed another Saturday session of stake conference in the three years of my service as a mission president. I feel that balanced the scales pretty well. And then there was this:

The Purest Kind of Church Work

There was a large amusement park in Nashville, Tennessee, called Opryland. I recall taking my family to this wonderland place once each year. Sometimes while walking though the park and watching my children run here and there to get on the rides or to see the shows, I would have come into my mind the thoughts of how, at that moment, I could be helping missionaries, or giving or preparing a talk. However, at such times I would smile and eat some more of my cotton candy and say to myself,. "Being with my family is church work." Then I'd feel better and move ever closer to a glorious future.

Perhaps that is the answer. Being with one's family is the highest form of church work—the best of all paths to a glorious future. The Church should have a report that needs to be sent in monthly upon which you would list the things you did that week with your family and the number of hours that it took to do so. The more hours on that side of the ledger, the more you sought the kingdom of God.

The family is at the heart of the kingdom of God. And church work is our way of helping to build the kingdom of God. Therefore, it follows, that time with the family is the truest form of church work.

And When You Are At Home

Most choices you will make in regards to the time you spend with your children will not be as dramatic as some of the ones I've described. Most choices pertaining to your involvement and interactions with your family will be in regards to what you do with them when you are at home. You can make the excuse that you are too tired to do things with the children like playing ball or going to the park. But you really aren't too tired. True, you are tired of what you have been doing at work. However, you are not tired of playing with the kids. The activities with them require a different source of energy than that which you have been engaged in at work. You still have plenty of energy for things like sitting with your children while they play video games and telling them, "Way to go!"

You could even play with them. Just don't try to win. That would mean that you are paying more attention to the game than you are to them. Playing ball with them, or board games, and having a sense of humor as you do so, will make a great impression on them. You know what I mean. Your positive and humorous attitude will make the time you spend with them rich for them and for you. Instead of taking energy from you, it will give energy to you. It is hard to imagine having a glorious future if you do not have a positive and cheerful outlook.

It is the little "day-to-day" activities and interactions that you have with your children before and after dinner (even a good time doing dishes and cleaning up) and the contact at bedtime that will make a continual impact on family happiness. These almost constant little things have a more powerful effect than trying to do big activities "once in a while." Remember that in the ballgame of family life, getting 365 singles in a year with your wife and children will be better than trying to get 24 home runs.

From time to time, just stand aside and look at your family and say to yourself, "To me these are the ones who will make the kingdom of God a piece of heaven for me." Then seek with all your heart to make that kingdom continue forever into your glorious future.

You respond, "You make me feel good by the things that you say. However, I'm not sure that all you say is true. I know a lot of good people, who seem to seek first the kingdom of God, and they still have really bad problems with their kids and in other aspects of their lives."

I reply, "Oh, you are right. There is no guarantee against disappointing, tragic, and sad things happening. That is the nature and blessings of this span of life called mortality. What I am saying is that as you seek first the kingdom of God, you will make it through these tough times and your sorrows will, in time, become joys."

"Tell me more."

"Read on."

CHAPTER 10

How Do I Know? My Life Tells Me So

You asked about the tragic and sad things that happen to good people. I'll do my best to respond to this question that has been asked by all of us at one time or another.

What Is A Glorious Future?

Notice that in this book we are talking about a "glorious future," not a "problem-free, stress-free future." It is in the struggle and in sensing the strength coming from God that the glorious aspects of life abound.

Not All Dreams Come True

I know that in all likelihood, you had more going for you in those days of becoming married than Marilyn and I had going for us. But these are not matters of comparison. It doesn't matter what is in the details. All that matters is the desire. What do you want in your marriage, in your life? Do you truly desire the kingdom of God?

I know full well that in matters of romantic love, some never find it. Or they find it and the person they love doesn't feel the same about them. Thus for one reason or another, some never marry.

Marilyn had a friend whom she had known in high school. Both she and this friend went on missions to England at the same time. This friend had a glorious mission. She was loved and respected by all the saints and members. Her desires were so right with the Lord. She truly sought the kingdom of God with all her heart.

Upon her return home, she became a school teacher. No man came along who won her love. She never married. She was a master schoolteacher. She had many nieces and nephews whom she adored as a mother adores her children. She was their confidant. She inspired them to goodness. She sang in the Tabernacle Choir for years. She served in the church and in the temple. Her life was rich and she blessed the lives of all she met. She truly sought the kingdom of God first in her life. She has received all "these other things."

Oh, sure, she would have liked to have been married. But she didn't sit around waiting for that to happen. She lived life to its fullest and she served the Lord with power and faith. She has had and continues to have a glorious future.

Some Dreams Get Broken

Others marry and their marriage falls onto hard times. Almost always it is because one of the two, or maybe both, began to seek the things of the world more than the kingdom of God. Their desires, perhaps only slightly, become fixed on something other than each other. They want things that supersede their desires to be together and to bless their family.

No Sure Fire Formulas

In telling this the following story, I know there are no simple answers. There are no certain formulas. What works for one couple or one family does not work for others. People are different and each problem is unique and each solution is hidden away in a different place.

Seldom is the solution on the surface crying out to be seen, but it is something that will require much effort to be found. One thing is certain:, if we seek first the kingdom of God, the outcome will be far better than we once thought that it could be.

Broken Things Can Be Fixed

In her youth, someone very close to me loved to consider her patriarchal blessing, which was filled with promises of a glorious future. The inspired words of this blessing promised that she and her husband would do much to help build the kingdom of God. When she married, she was ready to thrust in her sickle and to do all that she could to make all her promised blessings come true. She prayed and felt a witness that the young man with whom she had fallen in love could help her dreams and promises become realities.

However, in the early years of their marriage, her husband did not feel the same spiritual energy she felt. She tried to hold on. Children were born. He was being pulled away by the ways of the world. Finally, she could not endure his repeated failure to be faithful to the family. With no hope for a change, they went their separate ways.

She had never faced any problem nearly as difficult as this. Her heart was wounded in an almost irreparable way. But hope still burned within her. She fought with the urges to hide within the walls of her pain. Gradually she experienced more and more victories. Her once cast-down mood began to change. Light began to fill her countenance.

She challenged herself to do things that she had feared before. Always a fun-loving person, she extended her loving reach to all she met. She encouraged those who were suffering as she had suffered. Others began to seek her out to receive the strength that she could give. It was almost as if she was being compensated for injured feelings by receiving new, more wonderfully, sensitive feelings.

She cried much in private. Some problems require that. Tears came mostly at night in those dark hours that can be so long. Broken hearts do not heal easily. Perhaps they never do. Her early and frequently shed tears were not enough. As time passed these early tears were followed by less frequent, but never-failing times, that required additional inward sobbing.

Few knew of her sorrows, for she laughed much in public and all who knew her considered her to be among the happiest persons they had ever known. Gradually, even in her private moments, through the weeks, months, and years, the balance tilted more toward the laughter and less toward tears—more toward the excitement and fulfillment of the future than the pain of the past—more toward the glorious than toward the mundane.

In a very real sense, she found God in a new way. Her faith deepened. She knew His answers required His time table and His ways. She knew that promised blessings sometimes come in well-disguised packages. She knew that the seeking first the kingdom of God was not as easy as putting on a new set of clothes. Instead it required some pain, some suffering, and some patience to put on the garments that clothe the inward soul.

She counseled others and helped them to use their struggles as a means of coming to know an indescribably caring Father. Now, after some years, just to be in her presence gives one a glorious feeling. She is a bright light and all who know her seek her company. She has continued to move forward against great odds. It took all the courage she could muster to enroll in law school. In one more year she will be a lawyer.

When I told her the title I desired to use for this book I was writing—*A Glorious Future*—she sighed and asked, "Why could you not have written that earlier? Then perhaps I could have had a glorious future."

I looked at her radiant and beautiful face and exclaimed from the bottom of my heart, "I know of no other person who has made his or her way to such a glorious future as have you!"

If you knew her, and some of you do, your life would be blessed, for she truly has made her way through deep shadows and thorny paths to a glorious present and an even more glorious future.

Her story is her story. Your story is your story. She has found and continues to find her own unique answers. You must seek your own. However, she and you and all of us have one common overriding solution to aid us in gaining a glorious future—that universal answer that will lead us through a multitude of pain and joy is to seek first the kingdom of God. Then and only then, will "all these things" be added to you and to those you love.

When disappointment and sorrow do come to you, if you truly seek first the kingdom of God, you will grieve and shed your tears, and then you will decide to get on with your life. You will decide to do better than you have ever done before. If you make this decision and hang in there, things will get better than they have ever been. They always do.

A Time of Decision

I recall, in my own life, a time when my heart was not completely set to personally "seeking first the kingdom of God." I was in my second year of college, and had lost interest in pursuing, with real intent, my school work. I had also lost some interest in working, or any really good, self-improving cause.

My four friends and I were all in about the same boat. None of us were really going anywhere. So we mutually decided to join the Navy. I knew deep down that this was not a good choice for me. However, it was something to do and my friends encouraged me. So off we all went to Salt Lake City in Dale Astle's old car to join the Navy. My mother was not pleased with the decision, and told me so. I knew she was right, but it was my decision to make, not hers.

At the recruiting station we took our preliminary physical examinations. It was discovered that I had a minor physical problem that made it so I failed the exam. I was troubled by this. I really did not want to go in the Navy, but the rejection of even that possibility caused me to feel I was of no value to anyone.

By the time we had driven the 35 miles back home to American Fork, I was now extremely discouraged. My friends were excited to soon be sailors, and I was a reject.

I walked into the house. My mother was at the stove cooking. She spoke to me, but I did not reply. I went quickly to my bedroom and lay down with my face to the wall. I had never felt so lost.

After a time I heard my mother's voice, and I knew she was standing in the doorway. Just her voice enlivened a bit of hope in my heart. I knew that she would never reject me.

She asked softly, "How did it go?"

I did not reply. She asked, "When do you leave for the Navy?"

"I don't," I replied bluntly.

"Why?"

"Because I failed the physical. Nobody wants me for anything."

After a few seconds of silence, I could feel her sit on the bed.

She then said, "I'm making some chicken noodle soup. You love that. Why don't you come and eat, and we can talk?"

I did not want to talk, I wanted to cry.

She added, "George, I've been thinking. You could return to school. You could do better. I could help pay for it. You have so much you could do with your life. Now come on into the kitchen and eat. You'll feel better."

I was hungry and so I got up and followed her into the kitchen. Hope flooded into my heart. (It always does when we begin to consider doing better.) We didn't really talk. But just being there with her made me start to consider my life. Why not set out on a new course? Why not really get involved in the Church? Why not do what I ought to do?

A week later it was spring semester and I returned to school. This time I was ready. I took a new interest in the Church. I loved it. I started again to love life. To me the future began to look glorious.

Life is often a struggle. That is good. That is why we are here. Someday in your glorious future the Lord will say to you and your family, "Well done. Well done, indeed!" And you will reply, "Heavenly Father, you were right when you said, 'Seek ye first the kingdom of God, and his righteousness; and all these things shall be added unto you.'"

You reply to me, "You seem to have had a good life. However, you have been around quite awhile. How do you see your future as you come closer to the end of your days?"

THE LAST CHAPTER

The Sweetest Of All

I'm glad you asked about how we older folks feel about our future. A quick answer is, "I've never been as excited about my present and my future as I am now."

No wonder Lehi talked of the Tree of Life bearing the sweetest of all fruit. No other work could describe the feelings that come with "...all these things." Someone should write a hymn about the word "sweet." Perhaps it could go like this, "Sweet is the work..." But I don't know where it would go from there.

Oh, the glory of it all! What a wonderful kingdom is the kingdom of God! And to be part of it, right in the middle of it, goes beyond anyone's ability to describe. And it keeps getting better—more and more glorious. Where will it all end?

The Changing Vision of a Glorious Future

While at a temple wedding, you see the young couple beaming with happiness. Their hearts are filled with the hope of a glorious future. Sitting nearby are the grandparents and sometimes the great-grandparents. The hearts of these folks contain many memories of a glorious past. However, in their hearts there is still room for more . . . much, much more future mortal joy.

Perhaps the grandmother sitting off to the right is a widow. Maybe the elderly grandfather two rows back is a widower. Each of these two misses his or her departed mate with whom a glorious life has been shared. Each harbors in his or her heart a hope for a glorious reuniting with a departed sweetheart.

Two people, who are sitting close to each near the back of the room, are recalling their wedding of 55 years ago. They have among their most treasured future hopes those of seeing what good things will come next for their children, grandchildren, and great-grandchildren. They know that, along with the good times they will share in the next decade or two, there will come some pain and suffering and sorrow.

This couple and others of similar age, hope for many more years of mortal life. However, along with this hope, the reality of their mortal years gives them greater room in their hearts to extend their vision of a glorious future to a time that lies beyond mortality.

The hope of life beyond this one brings them joy and an almost eager excitement about how they will fit into the glorious spirit world, the resurrection, the Millennium, and the celestial world that has become such a real part in their inspired hearts.

They love the kingdom of God that they have been part of in this life. And they long to stay here. They also know of the kingdom of Heaven and they find hope and joy in looking forward to their place there when all the things promised by our Heavenly Father will be theirs.

The Stories Of Some Who Are Getting There

Big John Fugal

One of the most faithful followers of Christ whom I have ever known is John Fugal. He truly sought the kingdom of God first. He and his Elma have had such a glorious life. I recall in the late 1940s when John came to teach seminary in American Fork.

He was a tall, handsome, and impressive young man. He knew the word of the Lord, and he loved to teach it and to live it. In those days, it was obvious to all who knew him and his beloved new bride that they had a glorious future. And the hope they had then has grown and blossomed into all that God has promised.

Big John moved on through the years. He taught seminary for many seasons and then taught at BYU. Many young students were inspired by him to go on missions, to be married in the temple, and to seek first the kingdom of God. His faith was like a wildfire that reached out and burned its way into the hearts of a multitude.

Eventually Elma became ill. Then she worsened and went into the hospital. A grieving, but hopeful, John spent almost every waking hour at her bedside. Often he could be heard throughout the wing of the hospital reading aloud to Elma from the Book of Mormon.

Many people passing by listened to John's booming voice and were inspired. All were amazed by the tenderness of this faithful man and his eternal partner. They each sensed during this tragic experience that their days together on this earth were short, but their faith was long. The messages of the Book of Mormon reaffirmed to them that their glorious future together would be forever.

A few years have passed. John still comes to the temple often. It is a thrill to see him there. He sits among many. But there is one who, though not seen, sits at his side. She requires no chair. It is his beloved Elma.

As I see him there in the holy temple, I see that John's cheerful nature is undaunted. He still has much to live for. His children, grandchildren, and great-grandchildren add to his glorious present here on earth. But his heart yearns to be with Elma. And eventually he will be as he continues into his glorious future.

My Brother Stewart

My brother Stewart and his beautiful Leola lived into their nineties. To visit with them in their later years was like going into heaven to see those there. They have for so long sought the kingdom of God first. They have blessed the lives of so many. Finally the pains came to Leola. She suffered. She longed to go. Stewart brokenheartedly released her so she could be free from pain and go on to her glorious future.

Stewart visits her each week in the cemetery. I was at his house the other day when he came back from such a visit. He said to me. "I miss Leola. But I am glad she no longer suffers. Today she spoke to me as I stood by her graveside. She said, "Stewart, I like where I am now. It is a better place than American Fork, where we used to live, or Lehi, where you now live." Tears formed in his eyes and the light of hope made the tears glisten into a message of pure love.

"Stewart and Leola." I can't say one name without saying the name of the other, for they are not two—they are one. As I write this, my heart is full. I love my brother Stewart and his Leola. It won't be long until they will be together again in their glorious future.

I'm Getting There

Even I am growing a bit older. Sometimes that fact brings me sorrow and discouragement. I have had such a full life. I have always felt so young. Now as I write this book, I wonder, "Will this be my last book?" People used to ask me to come and speak at their meetings. They do not do that much anymore. I used to be a priesthood leader. Now I cheer for the younger men who have the joy of such service. I used to have such a pretty yard, and now it is a bit bedraggled. No matter how well those who are hired to care for our yard do, they can't do it like I used to do it. Marilyn has a hard time walking. She can't get out as much as she did in the past. So we stay home a lot.

Sometimes I get feeling that I look like I used to look many years ago, but then I see myself in the mirror and I know time has passed.

I talked to someone recently and they asked about things. I told them that we don't get out so much. I could tell that they pitied us. I told them to not do so. I told them of the love that has so settled into hearts of Marilyn and me. We just enjoy sitting and watching TV. Our favorite shows are home decorating shows or yard improvement shows. We store the ideas in our minds to be used on our mansions in heaven. We love to read out loud to each other. We love to pray. We love to go out to dinner each week with our son and his wife and our daughter. We love to get word from our children and grandchildren. We mention them in our every prayer.

Oh, sure, I miss the olden days—the glorious days when we were so challenged, the victories we won together, and the joy we shared with our young children, and on our missions and in Church service. But life is more sweet now than ever before. The people in our ward are so kind to us. We love to go to Church and see them. We love our home teachers. We love our bishop and we pray for him, his wife, and their family. We have no competitive feelings anymore. We want everyone to succeed. Everyone's success seems part of our success. We want all the marriages in our ward to last. We want all the children to thrive.

Some days I get discouraged. Walking helps. Writing helps. I paint water color paintings and that helps. I'm with Marilyn and that can push discouragement clear out of the window. Most of the time I'm happy. My prayers are more fervent now than ever before. I find I can pray away discouragement. Most of my prayer time is spent in asking the Lord to help others. Other than praying for good feelings, I feel guilty in praying for myself when others need my prayers so much more.

But overriding all this is the future. I really feel like Marilyn and I have and will continue to seek the kingdom of God first. We have had and continue to have a glorious life. And the future! How will it be to close this book of life and begin a whole new adventure in the spirit world? Oh, how exciting it will be! I can wait for it for a few more years because now life is so good, my love for Marilyn is so deep, and our children and grandchildren and great-grand children bring us such joy. But the way time flies by nowadays, I know that time will soon come. And when it does it will be glorious.

I used to say, "I do not want to die until the children are all raised." Then I changed and said, "I don't want to die until my grandchildren are all raised."

Now I say, "I do not want to die until my great-grandchildren are all raised." I just don't ever want to leave the family. And now I know that I don't have to die. I just have to go into the next room and wait. Pretty soon they will all come there and join Marilyn and me.

Oh, yes. The future will be so glorious—so very glorious.

Now my prayer is for you. Come all the way into the kingdom of God. Bathe yourself in its glory. Let your every motivation and longing be to seek the kingdom of God first.

Then just sit back and watch the miracles pour from the unlocked windows of heaven. Feel the Lord's power flow into your homes and hearts so as to almost knock you and those you love off your chairs with blessings.

Seek ye first the kingdom of God, and his righteousness; and all these things shall be added unto you. Matt 6:33

With love,
George Durrant